NEW MERMAIDS

General editors:
William C. Carroll, Boston University
Brian Gibbons, University of Münster
Tiffany Stern, University of Oxford

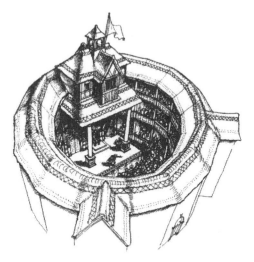

Reconstruction of an Elizabethan theatre
by C. Walter Hodges

NEW MERMAIDS

NEW MERMAIDS

FRANCIS BEAUMONT

THE KNIGHT OF THE BURNING PESTLE

2nd edition

edited by Michael Hattaway

Professor of English Literature
University of Sheffield

B L O O M S B U R Y

LONDON · NEW DELHI · NEW YORK · SYDNEY

Bloomsbury Methuen Drama

An imprint of Bloomsbury Publishing Plc

50 Bedford Square	1385 Broadway
London	New York
WC1B 3DP	NY 10018
UK	USA

www.bloomsbury.com

Bloomsbury is a registered trade mark of Bloomsbury Publishing Plc

First published New Mermaid Edition 1969 Ernest Benn Limited
Second Edition 2002
Reissued with a new cover design 2009
Reprinted 2012 (twice), 2013

Visit www.bloomsbury.com to find out more about our authors and their books
You will find extracts, author interviews, author events and you can sign up for
newsletters to be the first to hear about our latest releases and special offers.

British Library Cataloguing-in-Publication Data
A catalogue record for this book is available from the British Library.

ISBN: PB: 978-0-7136-5069-3
EPDF: 978-1-4081-4409-1
EPUB: 978-1-4081-4410-7

Library of Congress Cataloging-in-Publication Data
A catalog record for this book is available from the Library of Congress.

CONTENTS

ACKNOWLEDGEMENTS

Anyone who edits *The Knight of the Burning Pestle* must be grateful to predecessors, in my case to H. S. Murch and Cyrus Hoy for their editions of the play, and to theatre historians like Andrew Gurr who, in recent years, have refined greatly our understanding of the dramatic milieu. T. W. Craik and Roger Hardy supplied references for the first edition, Malcolm Jones for this one. In 1960 John Dawick invited me to act in a student production; later Brian Morris encouraged me to edit the play, Michel Bitot and Pierre Iselin rekindled my interest by invitations to lecture in France, and Brian Gibbons has overseen this revised edition with his customary insight and toleration. My son Rafe has observed my labours with a degree of quizzicality, my former student Judi Shepherd has given me inestimable support.

M. H.

INTRODUCTION

The Author

Francis Beaumont was born about 1585 in Leicestershire at Grace-Dieu, the country seat of his family. His grandfather and father had attained distinction as judges, and he evidently intended to continue the family tradition, for, having been admitted in 1597 as a gentleman commoner of Broadgates Hall (now Pembroke College), Oxford, in 1600 he left the university without taking a degree to become a member of the Inner Temple in London. Like many of his contemporary dramatists, his first publication was an erotic poem, *Salmacis and Hermaphroditus* (1602).[1] He had probably met John Fletcher by 1607 when they both published commendatory verses to Jonson's *Volpone*. In that year too Beaumont published his first play, *The Woman Hater*, a Jonsonian comedy of humours that satirises the prodigality of the aristocracy and which was performed by the Paul's Boys in the previous year. Between 1609 and 1611 the famous partnership with Fletcher was at its height, and during these years the King's Men, Shakespeare's company, performed their major collaborative works, *Philaster*, *The Maid's Tragedy*, and *A King and No King*. These plays are in fact the cornerstone of their joint reputation, for although their association is usually taken for granted, Beaumont probably had a hand in only about twelve of the fifty-two plays indiscriminately ascribed to both dramatists by the second folio collection of their works published in 1679. Alone or in collaboration with others, Fletcher went on writing for the stage until his death in 1625, but Beaumont seems to have retired from the stage about 1613 when he married Ursula Isley, the coheiress to a decayed Kentish house. He died on 6 March 1616, the same year as Shakespeare, and is buried in Westminster Abbey.[2]

Authorship and Date

Although three of the four seventeenth-century editions of the play attribute *The Knight of the Burning Pestle* to Beaumont and Fletcher, most modern critics, by means of an analysis of the play's unity of conception and of the style of its verse, have ascribed it to

---

[1] See below; it is reprinted in Sandra Clark, (ed.), *Amorous Rites: Elizabethan Erotic Verse*, (London, 1994), pp. 93–115.

[2] See Lee Bliss, *Francis Beaumont*, (Boston, 1987).

Beaumont alone. This ascription is convincingly supported by Cyrus Hoy's analysis of the linguistic habits of the authors who contributed to the Beaumont and Fletcher canon. The relevant evidence and argument, which centres on incidentals such as the authors' use of 'ye', third person singulars terminating in '-th', and contractions ('i'th', 'h'as', etc.), are set out in two important articles: 'The Shares of Fletcher and his Collaborators in the Beaumont and Fletcher Canon', (I) and (III), *Studies in Bibliography*, VIII and XI (1956 and 1958), 129–46 and 85–106.

The first edition of the play is a quarto dated 1613 (Q1). There is no mention of the author's name on the title-page, nor any indication of where the play had been performed. The *terminus ad quem* is therefore 1613, and the *terminus a quo* is 1607, the date of *The Travels of the Three English Brothers*, the latest of the plays referred to in the play. Within the text the three most important pieces of evidence for establishing the date more precisely are:

(i) The statements in the publisher's Epistle that he had 'fostered it privately' in his bosom 'these two years', and that it was the elder of *Don Quixote* 'above a year' (14–25). The first statement would imply that the play dates from 1611, likewise the second, for Shelton's translation of Cervantes' novel was entered on the Stationers' Register on 19 January 1610–11 and published in 1612. In all probability, however, the publisher, Burre, is referring not to the date of the first production, but to the date at which Robert Keysar, a goldsmith who financed the Children of the Revels, rescued the text from 'perpetual oblivion'. Keysar presumably provided Burre with a manuscript of the play sometime after it had become clear that the play would not do well in the theatre but after Beaumont had established his reputation. This part of the evidence therefore points to a date before 1611.

(ii) The Citizen remarks at IV, 49–50: 'Read the play of *The Four Prentices of London*, where they toss their pikes so'. The earliest surviving edition of this play is 1615. However, Fleay, in *A Biographical Chronicle of the English Drama* (London, 1891), i, 182, argued that the Citizen's reference is to a putative lost edition of 1610, for in the Epistle to the 1615 edition of *The Four Prentices* there is an allusion to the recent revival of the practice of arms in the Artillery Garden, a revival which, as Stow's continuator noted, occurred in 1610. Fleay accordingly dated the play 1610. His argument is, however, based on evidence which comes only from the Epistle, not from that part of the play which was acted. Moreover, in the same Epistle Heywood says the play was written 'in my infancy of judgement in this kind of poetry ... some fifteen or sixteen years ago', and an earlier part of this play, *Godfrey of Bulloigne*, had been entered on the Stationers' Register as early as

1594.[3] Finally, the context of the Citizen's remark is ironical as it suggests that he is treating a play which he had probably seen but not necessarily read as reliable 'history'.

(iii) The most important evidence, the Citizen's reference to 'This seven years there hath been plays at this house' (Induction, 6–7), which would fit almost exactly the years 1600–8 when the Children of the Revels were playing at the Blackfriars playhouse before it was taken over by the King's Men. Moreover the dedicatee is Robert Keysar, who had managed this troupe from about 1606.

The weight of the evidence therefore points to an original performance in 1607 or 1608, that is some seven years after the Children of the Revels had moved to Blackfriars. This is confirmed by the reference to Moldavia (IV, 58 and see IV, 34n.): the Prince of Moldavia was at Court in 1607. The other evidence for dating, the publication of some of Merrythought's songs in 1609, is inconclusive, as these were popular tunes and almost certainly known before their publication. If, however, the later date of 1610–11 is accepted, the play may have been performed at the short-lived Whitefriars where the Children of the Revels (again under Keysar) performed from 1609 to 1614.[4]

The Play

If the above argument is correct, *The Knight of the Burning Pestle* was written for the Blackfriars. This was one of London's private or hall playhouses where plays were presented indoors by (at this time) boy actors to an audience smaller than that of the public (amphitheatre) playhouses and where the price for admission was correspondingly higher. (It was in the private playhouses that the custom developed of viewing the play from stools on the stage.[5]) Analysis of the plays presented in the private theatres points to a taste there for parody or pastiche as well as intimate satire, and mannered if not truly sophisticated plays dealing with passionate intrigues of the sort that would appeal to the gentlemen of King James's Court.[6] Working from observations like these, most critics of *The Knight* have seen the essence of the play in what its first publisher called its

---

[3] Alfred Harbage, *Annals of English Drama 975–1700*, 3rd edn., (London, 1989), p. 107.

[4] Andrew Gurr, *The Shakespearian Playing Companies*, (Oxford, 1996), pp. 90, 117, 352–4.

[5] Andrew Gurr, *Playgoing in Shakespeare's London*, (Cambridge, 1987), p. 30.

[6] Gurr, *Playing Companies*, pp. 342–3, distinguishes between the satirical bite in the repertoire of the Blackfriars Boys and that of the Paul's Boys which celebrated citizen values.

'privy mark of irony'.[7] They take this to be its satire of the merchant class and of the citizens' taste for old-fashioned chivalric romance. Indeed, Alfred Harbage went so far as to argue that the play failed at its first presentation 'not because it satirised citizens [but] because it did so without animosity'.[8]

Yet a poem written by Jonson to Fletcher upon *The Faithful Shepherdess* (1608) reminds us that the censorious audience of the Blackfriars was not so homogeneous as to make it easy to argue that any play propounded the point of view of any particular social group:

> The wise and many-headed bench that sits
>   Upon the life and death of plays and wits
> (Composed of gamester, captain, knight, knight's man,
>   Lady or pucelle [whore], that wears mask or fan,
> Velvet or taffeta cap, ranked in the dark
>   With the shop's foreman, or some such brave spark
> That may judge for his sixpence) had, before
>   They saw it half, damned thy whole play, and more;
> Their motives were, since it had not to do
>   With vices, which they looked for, and came to.[9]

The high price of admission, sixpence, may have deterred the very poor who could gain admission to the amphitheatre playhouses for a penny,[10] but the poem delimits a wide social spectrum drawn from the more prosperous ranks of London society. Moreover, Beaumont's play satirises not only citizens but gallants, not only the militia but the gallery of roués in Barbaroso's 'cave', as well as the 'gentle' Humphrey, a would-be Paul's man (see V, 50). Satire in fact is incidental to the revelry which informs the play.

For, although *The Knight of the Burning Pestle* seems much concerned with the differences between the tastes of elite and non-elite groups, it is not simply snobbish, a burlesque which taunts citizens, their mentality, and their fantasies. The text activates brilliant contentions not only between different genres but between different kinds of representation. Within the text we see the improvisations of players set against authorial and company control. The patterns of popular or folk drama, in the form of a *Reihespiel* (episodic play) of the adventures of Rafe, are in competition and interwoven with the plottedness of a classical new comedy, 'The London Merchant',

---

[7] See his epistle to Robert Keysar, l. 5.

[8] Alfred Harbage, *Shakespeare and the Rival Traditions*, (New York, 1952), p. 108.

[9] Ben Jonson, *Poems*, ed. Ian Donaldson, (Oxford, 1975), p. 293; see also Gurr, *Playgoing*, pp. 93–5.

[10] Gurr, *Playgoing*, pp. 15–16.

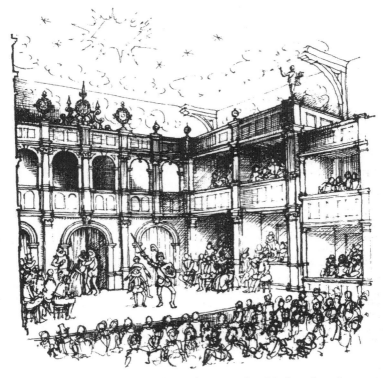

The Blackfriars Theatre drawn by C. Walter Hodges, based on
a reconstruction by R. Hosley and R. Southern.

performed by professionals – 'Plot me no plots', says George the Citizen (II, 268). Moreover, Beaumont makes no attempt to create a fictive world on the stage that spectators might 'believe in': rather he exploits the capacity of London playhouses not only to provide a space for theatrical games but to violate decorum or probability and accommodate in the same playing space both 'London' and the 'enchanted valley' (II, 105–6) of Waltham Down.[11] Sir Philip Sidney had castigated those who have 'Asia of the one side, and Afric of the other, and so many other under-kingdoms, that the player, when he cometh in, must ever begin with telling where he is, or else the tale will not be conceived'.[12] Beaumont, however, rejoices in this – or at least handles the matter subtly:

MISTRESS MERRYTHOUGHT
    Where be we now, child?
MICHAEL
    Indeed, forsooth, mother, I cannot tell, unless we be at Mile End. Is
    not all the world Mile End, mother?   (II, 67–9)

Beaumont's play extends its playing space beyond the on-stage stools for the gallants out to the auditorium and the audience themselves. That is the meaning of the brilliant moment at the opening when George and Nell, the Citizen and his Wife, come up onto the stage. By thus playing with dramatic conventions and widening the margins of theatrical experience, Beaumont anatomises the imaginative and behavioural codes of his society. 'All the world's a stage' is in some measure a motto for the baroque:[13] Beaumont enacts the notion by having the 'world' move onto the stage. The spectators too become players.
    Although the play sometimes pillories the taste of the citizens, it is significant that the on-stage gentlemen remain mute throughout the play. (This assumes that these bit parts were taken by players rather than spectators 'playing themselves'.) The implication is that they enjoy, tolerate, or (mere fops) are cowed by the exploits of Rafe, the usurping 'hero'. From this we deduce that the Blackfriars spectators were able to laugh at themselves as well as at rival class-attitudes in their society. Although the citizens, like the mechanicals

---

[11] See Robert Weimann, *Shakespeare and the Popular Tradition in the Theater*, ed. Robert Schwartz, (Baltimore, 1978), *passim* for the way in which stages functioned as both *platea* and *locus*, spaces for theatrical presentation and dramatic representation respectively.

[12] Philip Sidney, *An Apology for Poetry*, ed. G. Shepherd, (Manchester, 1965), p. 134.

[13] See P. Skrine, *The Baroque: Literature and Culture in Seventeenth-Century Europe*, (London, 1978), pp. 1–24.

in *A Midsummer Night's Dream*, on occasion take representation for reality, the text is not primarily concerned with this distinction. Rather it exhibits the spirit of what were termed in the early modern period 'revels', a hybrid category that was associated with seasonal activity, particularly carnival, and which included both dramatic performances and festive games in which spectators took as important a part as 'players'. In such contexts, drama as game is as important as drama as representation or mimesis, and all spectators are enjoined to take pleasure in and share the theatrical sports.

There are so many references to holiday festivities in the text that we might even postulate a Shrovetide or possibly Midsummer first performance – Beaumont's *Masque of the Inner Temple and Gray's Inn* was performed at Shrovetide, on 20 February 1613.[14] He had written his spoof *Grammar Lecture* for a feast when he was a student at the Inner Temple.[15] If this is the case, we could see the play in the context of seasonal community rituals which had survived edicts of reformation in the reign of Edward VI (1547–53) as well as those in the reign of Elizabeth (1558–1603).[16] 'Popular culture' in the period was not what Ronald Hutton calls 'a hermetically sealed entity'. He describes how close and complex the relationships were between 'printed and oral media, urban and rural communities, and different levels of the local and social hierarchy'.[17] Beaumont's play in fact might be an imaginative gesture within the art of theatre to an ideal of social communion. As we have seen, the publisher of Beaumont's text, Walter Burre, noted that the play's original spectators had failed to note the 'privy mark of irony' (Epistle, 5) in the text. Some construe this as having to do with the obvious satire of the citizenry, but if the play offers unvarnished portraits of them, it also recognises their strengths and celebrates a taste for romance shared by both gentry and citizens. Perhaps Beaumont was even deliberately attempting to construct a 'culture of consent',[18] to build bridges between court and city. The final song of the play hints at social discord as a cause of individual discontent:

---

[14] Francis Beaumont and John Fletcher, *The Dramatic Works in the Beaumont and Fletcher Canon*, ed. Fredson Bowers, (Cambridge, 1966–96), 10 vols., I, p. 113.

[15] Mark Eccles, 'Francis Beaumont's *Grammar Lecture*', *Review of English Studies*, 16 (1940), 402–14.

[16] François Laroque, *Shakespeare's Festive World*, trans. Janet Lloyd, (Cambridge, 1991); Ronald Hutton, *The Rise and Fall of Merry England: The Ritual Year 1400–1700*, (Oxford, 1994).

[17] Ronald Hutton, 'The English Reformation and the Evidence of Folklore', *Past and Present*, 148 (1995), 89–116, at 112.

[18] Peter Stallybrass, '"Wee feaste in our Defense": Patrician Carnival in Early Modern England and Robert Herrick's "Hesperides"', *ELR*, 16 (1986), 234–52, at 236–7.

> *Better music ne'er was known*
> *Than a choir of hearts in one.*
> *Let each other that hath been*
> *Troubled with the gall or spleen,*
> *Learn of us to keep his brow*
> *Smooth and plain as ours are now.*
> *Sing, though before the hour of dying;*
> *He shall rise, and then be crying,*
> *'Hey, ho, 'tis nought but mirth,*
> *That keeps the body from the earth'.*   (V, 342–51)

Some years later the Duke of Newcastle wrote to Charles II urging him to support 'honest pastime, harmless mirth ... There should be plays to go up and down the country. The divertissements will amuse the people's thoughts, and keep them in harmless action which will free your ma[jes]ty from faction and rebellion.'[19] In the end the delight at Rafe's achievements may create a kind of social cohesiveness in the playhouse, which, according to Keith Thomas, was one of the roles of laughter in the early modern period.[20]

The title of Beaumont's play takes off from court plays of the Elizabethan period, heroical romances with titles like *The Knight of the Golden Shield* (1570) or *The Knight of the Burning Rock* (1579),[21] but although it may parody their conventions and gently mock a naive attitude towards the kinds of illusion they deployed, it conjures their spirit. Those court plays obviously had themselves derived from 'popular' romances. Whether they laced romance with wit or a kind of theatrical self-consciousness we do not know: a few years later George Peele thought fit to define his theatrical art by affixing an induction peopled with three pages, Antic, Frolic, and Fantastic, to *The Old Wive's Tale* (1593), a court play belonging to the Queen's Men. Whatever Francis Beaumont's implied intentions may be, theatrical experience of modern productions demonstrates that, like Don Quixote, Rafe is as much hero as noddy, and that the play in performance kindles the innocent pleasures of revelry, of sympathy and delight. There may be laughter at the expense of the citizens, but it is not the kind of ridicule to be encountered in Cavalier circles later in the seventeenth century. This response is not only because of Rafe's aptitude as a player, albeit an amateur one,

---

[19] 'The Duke of Newcastle on Government', *A Catalogue of Letters ... at Welbeck*, ed. S. A. Strong, (London, 1903), p. 227, cit. Stallybrass, p. 239.

[20] Keith Thomas, 'The place of laughter in Tudor and Stuart England', *TLS*, 21 January (1977), 77–81. Alternatively we might see it as yet another Jacobean evocation of a lost 'Merry England'; compare George Chapman, *Bussy d'Ambois* (1604–5), I.ii.1–38; Shakespeare and Fletcher, *King Henry VIII* (1613), V.iv.

[21] See Harbage, *Annals*.

but because he is no loser – he *does* do 'admirable things' (Induction, 35). Although he may have been knocked down by Jasper, roles become reversed. He robustly defeats the barber, plays the role of a kind of leveller, and seizes the moment: 'Presumptuous man, see to what desperate end / Thy treachery hath brought thee' (III, 351–2). He also, with the help of George and Nell, subverts the plot.

Of course we can only infer how the play was read at those early Blackfriars performances, but there is a record of a comparable revel that was written during the Commonwealth and which is full of nostalgia for the way the dramatic sports of Merry England served to overcome distinctions of class (as well as those of gender):

> Such strange impressions makes strong fancies, and works not only upon women wonderful effects, but even the most masculine spirits have been (as well as our Don) shrewdly tainted with it. A gentleman [was] importuned, at a fire-night in the public hall, to accept the high and mighty place of a mock-emperor, which was duly conferred upon him by seven mock-electors at the same time, with much wit and ceremony. The emperor ascended his chair of state, which was placed upon the highest table in the hall, and at his instalment all pomp, reverence, and signs of homage were used by the whole company. Insomuch that our emperor (having a spice of self-conceit before, was soundly peppered now) for he was instantly metamorphosed to the stateliest, gravest, and commanding soul that ever eye beheld. Taylor acting Arbaces or Swanston D'Ambois were shadows to him; his pace, his look, his voice, and all his garb was altered. Alexander upon his elephant, nay upon the castle upon that elephant, was not so high; and so close did this imaginary honour stick to his fancy that for many years he could not shake off this one night's assumed deportments until the times came that drove all monarchical imaginations out, not only of his head but everyone's.[22]

A 'fire-night'[23] was almost certainly Midsummer Eve or St Peter's Eve (28 June). John Stow considered these occasions as having two functions. As well as 'to purge the infection of the air', they served to promote good amity: 'These were called bonfires, as well of amity amongst neighbours, that being before at controversy, were thereby by the labour of others reconciled, and made of bitter enemies, loving friends'.[24] The author's *Survey of London* celebrated

---

[22] Edmund Gayton, *Pleasant Notes upon Don Quixot*, (London, 1654), pp. 24–5.

[23] The word is not recorded in *OED*.

[24] Stow, I, p. 101.

the honour of the capital's citizens by offering elaborate accounts of its ritualised ceremonies and revelries.[25]

The Knight of the Burning Pestle is one of many early modern plays that takes place within a frame. It has an Induction – although it is not called that in the first quarto. That Induction seems to be occupied by members of the playing company, the Children of the Revels playing at Blackfriars, but their theatrical time and space are, as we have seen, invaded by members of the audience, the Citizen and his household. This theatrical insurrection is crucial to understanding the play, both its mode and its historical location. Gayton reminded us of how mock insurrections, 'monarchical imaginations', prefigured real ones: *The Knight of the Burning Pestle* would be ruined if we were to interpret it as much more than a divertissement, and yet it does bear comparisons with inversionary rituals and seasonal riots of the sort that have drawn the attention of critics and cultural historians. Not only do the Citizens require a heroic mode and emblems of chivalry to authenticate their social status, but they demand folk revelry, part of the collective consciousness of the nation, aspects of which groups of puritans were trying to suppress. Fantasies or what Francis Bacon called 'idols of the tribe' *do* have a part to play in the collective experience: to deny them makes spectators of a 'puritan disposition' as one-eyed as Don Quixote himself.

To return to the Induction: among the boys is a Prologue – a player who takes that named part.[26] We should expect the Epilogue to be reappropriated by 'players', members of the Revels 'company', but in fact the lines of the Epilogue are spoken by the Citizen and his wife. The dramatic frame turns out to function rather like a Möbius strip. George and Nell take over the occasion and, as in classical comedy, *The Shoemaker's Holiday*, and *Bartholomew Fair*, end the play with an invitation to dinner.

There are in fact three groups of characters, three plot lines: that concerning the Citizen, the play of 'The London Merchant', and the improvised series of episodes that depict Rafe's adventures and self-fashionings. Characters from 'The London Merchant', Mistress Merrythought, et al., encounter Rafe and become part of his story. 'The London Merchant' would resemble a formulaic domestic comedy based on Venturewell as the patriarch (*senex*) unsympathetic to his daughter's true love and Jasper as the ironic hero, were it not for the romantic adventures involving Mistress Merrythought and her son Michael. Rafe's role is both presentational and repre-

---

[25] See Lawrence Manley, *Literature and Culture in Early Modern London*, (Cambridge, 1995), pp. 159–61.

[26] This is to be distinguished from the 'Prologue', a text taken from Lyly's *Sappho and Phao* that is found in the Prefatory matter to Q2.

sentational: the fact that this is encouraged by the Citizen and his wife suggests that 'popular drama' has dramatic conventions that may be more complex than the demands for 'realism' made by proponents of academic or coterie drama.

As the play progresses Rafe's acting must change as he undergoes a kind of metamorphosis from prentice-hero to Lord of Misrule.[27] Such figures were common in May-games as well as Christmas and Shrovetide festivities. According to London's chronicler John Stow, Lords of Misrule made 'the rarest pastimes to delight the beholders',[28] and it is worth remembering how, in aristocratic entertainments, the Lord of Misrule or Master of the Revels was likely to be an aristocratic amateur rather than a professional player. Rafe's triumph thus represents the triumph of the non-professional – he had previously acted the 'huffing' parts (Induction, 75) of Mucedorus and Shakespeare's Prince Hal – over the professional. Although the pretensions of the Citizens to be members of a society that lived by codes of honour are mocked, their evocation of chivalry is coloured by a kindly nostalgia which the audience is invited to share. The Citizen bears the name of England's saint, yet St George and the Dragon were to be found 'only on tavern- or inn-signs'[29] and in memories of 'ridings' and civic pageants suppressed by the reformers. As Lord of Misrule, Rafe is able to direct the attention of the audience to the absurdities of the play they had come to see. We might even see the whole play as an endorsement, for a court audience, of the delights of inversionary laughter, of those holy days and seasonal games, particularly those associated with Shrovetide, as well as fire-nights and May-poles, which 'Puritans' of the age like Philip Stubbes and his successors (see below) were trying to stamp out. In fact a rash of sabbatarians who inveighed against these things emerged between 1603 and 1608, although this complaint literature well-nigh vanished soon after the play's first performance.[30]

The use of the word 'metamorphosis' above is deliberate since 'Salmacis and Hermaphroditus', Beaumont's early erotic epyllion or verse romance, was based on episodes of disguise and Ovidian transformation. In the verse Epistle to the work, like the play a mingle-mangle of styles, Beaumont notes the capacity of the poem to transform the reader:

---

[27] See Hutton, *Merry England*, pp. 9–12, 60, 116–17; Charles Phythian-Adams, 'Ceremony and the Citizen: The Communal Year at Coventry 1450–1650', in *Crisis and Order in English Towns 1500–1700: Essays in Urban History*, ed. Peter Clark and Paul Slack, (London, 1972), pp. 57–85, at p. 67.

[28] Cited Hutton, *Merry England*, p. 9.

[29] Laroque, p. 111.

[30] Hutton, *Merry England*, pp. 55, 98–9, 156.

The title-page of Ortuñez de Calahorra's
Espejo de Principes y Caualleros (*The Mirror of Knighthood*)

I hope my poem is so lively writ,
That thou wilt turn half-maid with reading it.

There is a similar theme in Marston's exercise in this genre, 'The Metamorphosis of Pygmalion's Image' (1598), which concentrates not so much on the metamorphosis of the statue-maid into living woman but on the artist/spectator, enamoured of and transformed by his art, changed in that instance from misogynist to lover. Watching the exploits of Rafe we too are flaunted out of any sceptical or anti-romantic humour that may possess us: *we* become changelings. *The Knight of the Burning Pestle* actually recreates us as an audience – makes us aware of our roles.

Rafe's standing in the eyes of the audience is also defined by the dramatic mode within which he acts. As the chief player in the romantic chronicle, Rafe is defined against the world of 'The London Merchant'. It is not the case, however, that this part of the play creates a positive term. (This claim is borne out by the fact that we now know that the repertories, textual modalities, and audiences of public and private playhouses were more similar than used to be thought.) The play does not set up the worlds of 'realism' and illusion, the workaday and the romantic, the worlds of Sancho Panza and Quixote, as opposites. We see this by inspecting the mode or style of 'The London Merchant'. George need not in fact have worried: this is *not* a play that 'girds at citizens' (Induction, 8). It is not at all like 'citizen comedy', the satire of Middleton or Jonson, but itself far more a romance in the style of Dekker's *Shoemaker's Holiday* (1599). This drama that the grocers interrupt also subverts itself by its mode of travesty or genial pastiche[31] – there is play between Luce and Jasper on words like 'plot', 'part', and 'perform' (I, 56–8)[32] that recalls the inductions to plays by John Marston. The Merchant is called 'Venturewell': there is a parallel between this merchant adventurer and the adventures of the grocer's prentice.[33] 'The London Merchant' models itself upon the pattern of new comedy with a hero or *eiron* rescuing his love from an inflexible and fossilised society, peopled with *alazons* or

---

[31] Compare Manley: '*The London Merchant* only becomes an antiromantic citizen comedy, in other words, to the extent that the citizens' perspective makes it so. ... Beaumont's play is not simply a satire on bourgeois tastes and values but an essay on comedy...' (p. 468).

[32] Glenn A. Steinberg, '"You know the plot / We both agreed on": Plot, Self-consciousness, and *The London Merchant* in Beaumont's *The Knight of the Burning Pestle,*' *MARDIE*, 5 (1991), 211–24.

[33] For the 'neo-feudal tenor of the civic ethos ... in popular myths extolling London's merchant-heroes', see Manley, pp. 129–30.

hypocritical noddies.[34] It also inverts the pattern of the prodigal
son plays[35] – although Nell does not see this, choosing to support
the fatuous Humphrey. It parodies the sort of coincidence found
in romance and mocks ghost scenes from plays like *Macbeth*.[36] It
may also contain remnants of the kind of folk-drama that, as we
shall see, informs the Rafe episodes. Mistress Merrythought, as
gullible in her way as Nell, alludes to a ritual play, a mock-battle,
as a reality:

> Mile End is a goodly matter; there has been a pitch-field, my child,
> between the naughty Spaniels and the Englishmen; and the Spaniels
> ran away, Michael, and the Englishmen followed. My neighbour
> Coxstone was there, boy, and killed them all with a birding-piece.
>   (II, 71–5)

Merrythought is in some ways another Lord of Misrule, the master
of the wassail bowl (II, 441) – 'The London Merchant' itself contains elements of carnival.[37] It is also possible that, like Nell,
Mistress Merrythought has something in her of the unruly woman
that we associate with the victims of skimmingtons and other forms
of inversion ritual. Merrythought, she proclaims, 'shall never come
between a pair of sheets with me again while he lives' (II, 79–80) –
although her rebellion peters out rather pathetically.[38] Illusion here

---

[34] See Northrop Frye, 'The argument of comedy', *English Institute Essays*, (1948),
and Leo Salingar, *Shakespeare and the Traditions of Comedy*, (Cambridge, 1974).

[35] The heroine of *The London Prodigal* (1603–4) performed by the King's Men was
also called Luce.

[36] Stanley Wells, 'Staging Shakespeare's Ghosts', *The Arts of Performance in
Elizabethan and Early Stuart Drama: Essays for G. K. Hunter*, ed. Murray Briggs,
et al., (Edinburgh, 1991), 50–69.

[37] For wassailing, see Hutton, *Merry England*, pp. 13–14; for other examples of
singing humours, see Charles Read Baskervill, *The Elizabethan Jig and Related
Song Drama*, (Chicago, 1929), p. 161. Merrythought may also be related to the
vices who livened up Tudor Interludes. In John Rastell's *The Four Elements* (c
1517–18), 'Sensual Appetite' enters singing a jumble of clichéd popular refrains:
'*Make room, sirs, and let us be merry, / With 'huffa galant' sing, tirl on the berry,
/ And let the wide world wind! / Sing, frisky jolly, with hey troly lolly.*' See Tessa
Watt, *Cheap Print and Popular Piety, 1550–1640*, (Cambridge, 1991), p. 31;
'huffa galant' was a call used in falconry.

[38] Natalie Z. Davis, 'Women on Top', *Society and Culture in Early Modern France*,
(Stanford, 1975), pp. 124–51. The oath Luce swears to marry only a man who has
stolen her away (I, 187–8) may contain a reference to Hock Monday ceremonies
in which men bound up women before roles were reversed on Hock Tuesday (see
Phythian-Adams, pp. 68–9).

as elsewhere does not equal imitation: rather a drawing of the audience into the play between and among codes of representation.

So although the play might seem to be mocking the conventions of and taste for chivalric romance, it does not do this by erecting the pointed satire of a citizen comedy as a positive. The first age of neochivalric prose romances might have coincided with the age of Sidney and Spenser, but texts of this kind continued to be produced throughout the seventeenth century.[39]

What we have within the play's frame is the theatrical equivalent of a series of ritualised riots, analogous to the holiday rampages of the prentices at Shrovetide or the Christmas or Shrovetide practice of 'barring-out' at schools when pupils, their requests for holiday having been denied, locked their masters out of the school. Sometimes these occasions could turn brutal; at other times they attracted invited governors, parents, and townsfolk who were supplied with cakes and ale.[40] The play's structure invokes this theatricalised behaviour outside of the playhouse that depended upon audience collusion. The first insurrection is the invasion of the theatre itself. The second may well be a rebellion by another unruly woman, Nell, who interrupts her husband George's pompous request for 'something notably in honour of the of the commons of the city' (Induction, 26–7) with her robust 'Let him kill a lion with a pestle, husband; let him kill a lion with a pestle' (Induction, 43–4). And Nell, although played by a male actor, has appeared in the audience and is seemingly a 'real' woman when she storms a stage peopled entirely by men. She then delivers a ringing rebuke to Merrythought for the treatment of his wife:

WIFE

I had not thought, in truth, Master Merrythought, that a man of your age and discretion, as I may say, being a gentleman, and therefore known by your gentle conditions, could have used so little respect to the weakness of his wife. For your wife is your own flesh, the staff of your age, your yoke-fellow, with whose help you draw through the mire of this transitory world ...

OLD MERRYTHOUGHT ([*sings*] *within*)

I come not hither for thee to teach,

---

[39] Margaret Spufford, *Small Books and Pleasant Histories: Popular Fiction and its Readership in Seventeenth-Century England*, (Cambridge, 1981), pp. 232–7; see also Helen Moore, 'Romance', in *A Companion to English Renaissance Literature and Culture*, ed. Michael Hattaway, (Oxford, 2000), pp. 317–26. Sidney's *Arcadia* provided the plot for Day's *The Isle of Gulls* acted at the Blackfriars the year before *The Knight of the Burning Pestle*.

[40] See Keith Thomas, *Rule and Misrule in the Schools of Early Modern England*, (Reading, 1976), p. 25.

> *I have no pulpit for thee to preach,*
> *I would thou hadst kissed me under the breech,*
> *As thou art a lady gay.*

And Nell retorts: 'Give me such words that am a gentlewoman born! Hang him, hoary rascal! Get me some drink, George, I am almost molten with fretting: now beshrew his knave's heart for it' (III, 538–55).[41]

Another social category important for an understanding of the play is that of the apprentice. As now, adolescents constituted a social category in early modern London, and there is some evidence that schoolboys (like the Children of the Revels) were warned against them.[42] In London their standing as a group was registered by regular riots on Shrove Tuesday. The following account of these occasions and of popular theatrical taste is taken from Gayton's memories of a play by Ben Jonson:

... the comedy wanted not its *prodesse et delectare*, had it been exhibited to a scholastic confluence; yet men come not to study at a playhouse but love such expressions and passages which with ease insinuate themselves into their capacities ... on holy days, when sailors, watermen, shoemakers, butchers, and apprentices are at leisure, then it is good policy to amaze those violent spirits with some tearing tragedy full of fights and skirmishes: as *The Guelfs and Guiblins*, *Greeks and Trojans*, or *The Three London Apprentices* which commonly ends in six acts, the spectators frequently mounting the stage and making a more bloody catastrophe amongst themselves than the players did. I have known upon one of these festivals, but especially at Shrovetide, where the players have been appointed, notwithstanding their bills to the contrary, to act what the major part of the company had a mind to: sometimes *Tamburlaine*, sometimes *Jugurth*, sometimes *The Jew of Malta*, and sometimes parts of all these, and at the last, none of the three taking, they were forced to undress and conclude the day with *The Merry Milkmaids*. And unless this were done, and the popular humour satisfied, as sometimes it so fortuned that the players were refractory, the benches, the tiles, the lathes, the stones, oranges, apples, nuts flew about most liberally; and as there were mechanics of all professions who fell every one to his own trade and dissolved the house in an instant and made a ruin of a stately fabric. It was not then the most mimical or fighting man, Fowler nor Andrew Cane, could pacify; prologues nor epilogues

---

[41] For the exclusion of women from the plays and ceremonies of the craft guilds, see Phythian-Adams, p. 59.

[42] Steven R. Smith, 'The London Apprentices as Seventeenth-Century Adolescents,' *Past and Present*, 61 (1973), 149–61; Thomas, *Rule and Misrule*, p. 6.

would prevail; the devil and the fool were quite out of favour. Nothing but noise and tumult fills the house, until a cog take'em, and then to the bawdy-houses and reform them, and instantly to the Bankside where the poor bears must conclude the riot and fight twenty dogs at a time beside the butchers, which sometimes fell into the service. This performed, and the horse and jackanapes for a jig, they had sport enough that day for nothing.[43]

The relevance of events like these to *The Knight of the Burning Pestle* is obvious.

The play is also positioned within the context of festival and festivity by Rafe's May Lord speech. May-games were associated with sexual transgression, as his obnoxiously cute lines remind us:

> The lords and ladies now abroad for their disport and play,
> Do kiss sometimes upon the grass, and sometimes in the hay.
> (Interlude IV, 41–2)

Rafe also evokes the morris dancers – on occasion they figured in London guild pageants.[44] Although the text suggests nothing of the wild and primitive that we encounter in Shakespeare's description of Jack Cade as a 'wild Morisco' (*2 Henry VI*, III.i.365), it is conceivable that the speech in performance was accompanied by other actors playing Robin Hood, the hobby-horse, even a licentious Maid Marion. The Citizen hints as much by saying that dancing the Morris may prove 'too much for the boy' (Interlude IV, 24). In his Shrovetide *Masque of the Inner Temple and Gray's Inn*,[45] Beaumont 'chose to parody the dance by adding a pair of fools and of baboons. They "capered rudely" and the audience drowned the music with its laughter. Likewise when in 1617 Barten Holyday had a morris to represent Music in an allegorical play about the arts, he included a clowning hobby-horse, which knocked over the other performers'.[46]

What is significant about these occasional riots is that the prentices attacked the very institutions, playhouses, brothels, and bear-baitings, that their parents and masters abhorred – James Harrington was to write of 'their ancient administration of justice

---

[43] Gayton, p. 271; on Shrove Tuesday 1617 a mob of apprentices was to sack the Blackfriars (*The Letters of John Chamberlain*, ed. N. E. McClure, 2 vols., (Philadelphia, 1939), II, pp. 59–60).

[44] Peter Burke, *Popular Culture in Early Modern Europe*, (London, 1978), p. 78; Hutton, *Merry England*, pp. 33, 61.

[45] Beaumont and Fletcher, *Dramatic Works*, I, p. 133.

[46] Hutton, *Merry England*, p. 166.

at Shrovetide'.[47] In his ghost speech Rafe specifically conjures the Shrove Tuesday disorders:

> Farewell, all you good boys in merry London;
> Ne'er shall we more upon Shrove Tuesday meet
> And pluck down houses of iniquity.   (V, 327–9)

An analogy is therefore evoked: the Citizens destroy a dull play, overthrow academic decorum, attack the authority of playwright and players. It is not a question of unruliness but of misruliness.[48] Is, however, their 'riot' 'contained'?

The riot is not only material – the occupation of the playhouse – but aesthetic: an alien genre is imposed upon the theatrical offering. We can locate four such: Rafe's wooing of Princess Pompiona of Moldavia (IV, 57–124), the May Lord sequence (Interlude IV, 27–62), the muster at Mile End (V, 89–159), and Rafe's ghost scene (V, 284–335). These belong not just to seasonal ritual[49] but to specific patterns of folk drama. It might also be the case that the fight with the Barber owes as much to folk 'Hero combats' as to Cervantes. Specific records of such performances in England are lacking, although there is much evidence of revels activity in the records of municipal guilds. They obviously had ceremonial 'harness' (armour) which appeared in Midsummer Watches,[50] as well as stores of costumes which were hired out, even if these were used only on pageant wagons. They also provided giants for Midsummer Shows, and at Chester on 21 May 1601 the Drapers presented a play of Balaam and Balaam's Ass.[51] In the text itself we learn that Rafe, himself a player for the Company of Grocers, has played 'Mucedorus before the wardens of [the Grocers'] Company' (Induction, 84). Perhaps these secular entertainments took the place of the religious cycles, especially those associated with Corpus Christi but suppressed in the 1570s. There is some evidence of performances of very similar sequences by guilds in Germany and

---

[47] James Harrington, *The Commonwealth of Oceana and A System of Politics*, ed. S. B. Liljegren, (Lund, 1924), p. 152; further examples are to be found in Hutton, *Merry England*, p. 188; see also François Laroque, *Shakespeare's Festive World*, trans. Janet Lloyd, (Cambridge, 1991), pp. 96–103.

[48] Phythian-Adams, p. 67.

[49] Jackson I. Cope, *The Theater and the Dream: From Metaphor to Form in Renaissance Drama*, (Baltimore, 1973), pp. 201–10; Francis Beaumont, *The Knight of the Burning Pestle*, ed. Sheldon P. Zitner (Manchester, 1984), p. 41.

[50] R. W. Ingram, (ed.), *Records of Early English Drama: Coventry* (Manchester, 1981), *passim*.

[51] Lawrence M. Clopper, (ed.), *Records of Early English Drama: Chester* (Manchester 1979), p. 206.

France, associated with Shrovetide. 'The early *Fastnachtsspiele* are often constructed, in whole or in part, as a *Reihespiel* (or *Revue)*: "a simple sequence of separate comic speeches". At its most elementary, the *Reihespiel* consists of a number of quite unrelated speeches, usually of equal length, by a number of characters who step forward one after another and address the audience directly, without reference to or interaction with each other. Each speech is usually little more than a self-dramatisation of the speaker'.[52] It is characteristic of such sequences that the player describes himself:

> With gilded staff and crossèd scarf, the May-lord here I stand
> (Interlude IV, 34)

and

> grim cruel Death met me again,
> And shot this forkèd arrow through my head   (V, 323–4)

It is possible that the Pompiona sequence incorporates familiar episodes from *Fastnachtsspiele*, in which a series of male characters woos a lady. Rafe may have come in on his hobby-horse: wooing a lady was also a motif in morris dances.[53]

He also reviews the muster at Mile End, playing the role of a 'chosen city captain' (V, 307) – the equivalent of an elected Lord of Misrule or Boy Bishop in youth-abbeys or youth-kingdoms.[54] The speech ends with an injunction to seek out the 'enemy within': 'Remember, then, whose cause you have in hand, and like a sort of true-born scavengers, scour me this famous realm of enemies' (V, 153–5) which reminds us of how Rafe 'prolonged' his May-lord speech with a patriotic prayer: 'God save our king, and send his country peace, / And root out treason from the land! And so, my friends, I cease' (Interlude IV, 61–2). Other parts of his speech, however, are joyously bawdy: weapons are phallic, and 'touch-holes' run and stink with a metaphorical pox. This whole episode too may derive from seasonal revelry – the scene is very similar to a passage in John Taylor's *Jack-a-Lent* describing Shrovetide riots:

> Then Tim Tatter (a most valiant villain) with an ensign made of a piece of baker's mawkin [mop used to clean out a baker's oven] fixed upon a broom-staff, he displays his dreadful colours and, calling the

---

[52] Thomas Pettitt, 'English Folk Drama and the Early German *Fastnachtsspiele*', *Renaissance Drama*, n.s. 13, (1982), 1–34 at 14.

[53] Pettitt, 'English Folk Drama'; Hutton, *Merry England*, p. 61.

[54] Natalie Z. Davis, *Society and Culture in Early Modern France*, (Stanford, 1975), p. 110.

ragged regiment together, makes an illiterate oration stuffed with a most plentiful want of discretion the conclusion whereof is that somewhat they will do, but what they know not. Until at last comes marching up another troop of tatterdemalions, proclaiming wars against no matter who, so they may be doing ... [55]

Aggressive tribal nationalism has scarcely disappeared today: these 'troops' are like rioting football fans, and, specifically, Rafe's 'Hey for our town' (Interlude IV, 54) evokes the way in which the Morris dance served 'as a vehicle of competitive sport between different villages'.[56] The final episode, the ghost speech, is amiably ridiculous in that Rafe enters as a ghost, speaks lines that parody a variety of heroic plays,[57] and then 'dies' again. (A precise puritan might detect an allusion to the purgatory of popular unreformed religion.) There may be an analogy with the miraculous cures performed in folk drama of which a shadow may remain in *Doctor Faustus* (Scene xiii) where the hero revives after being beheaded at the court of the German Emperor.[58] In our play the difference between character and player – Rafe dies as one and revives as the other – is characteristically elided.

There are, then, in this play, no positive terms. Aesthetic energy circulates between the pastiche text of 'The London Merchant' and the festive and folk plays associated with the Citizens. It may be fitting therefore to end at the beginning, with the first three lines of the play, which contain a punctuation crux:

> From all that's near the court, from all that's great[,]
> Within the compass of the city-walls,
> We now have brought our scene –   (Induction, 1–3)

The lines can mean either that the company have given a local habitation and a name to fantasies and romance, or have relocated within the liberty of the Blackfriars, itself within the city, all that is courtly and magnificent. It turns on a possible comma at the end of the first line, and it is impossible to decide whether one should be included or not. Our reading of this text has to remain indeterminate, because the play is Janus-faced, tinged with nostalgia for Merry England, but aware of the way the energies of the individu-

---

[55] John Taylor, 'Jack-a-Lent', *Works*, (London, 1630), reprinted by Spenser Society (London, 1868–9), p. 115; the passage is discussed by N. Rhodes, *Elizabethan Grotesque*, (London, 1980), pp. 16–17.

[56] Laroque, p. 135.

[57] Beaumont, *The Knight*, V, 277 s.d., 278 nn.

[58] Thomas Pettitt, 'The Folk-Play in Marlowe's *Doctor Faustus*', *Folklore* 91 (1980), 72–7.

alist hero, once the prerogative of England's gentle knights, were being rapidly appropriated for her city merchants. And, by 1607–8, was there really a difference?

Stage History

As we have seen, the play was first performed in one of the fashionable Jacobean 'private' playhouses that catered to the wealthier sections of the London population. As in the 'public' or amphitheatre playhouses, all acting parts were taken by males, but in the first years of the seventeenth century the companies were composed of boys rather than men. Discrepancies between the age and gender of the boy players and those of the parts they took as well as the visibility of musicians and the comparative intimacy of the hall theatres may have encouraged bravura playing, created a kind of mannerism,[59] and it is common for the plays performed in these playhouses to begin with inductions studded with allusions which flatter the spectators into thinking they constitute a coterie and draw attention to the theatrical strategies of what is to follow. However, theatrical self-consciousness was a feature of much early modern drama[60] and precise evidence for distinctive playing styles is impossible to find.

As with acting so with staging: there is no evidence that staging was more elaborate in private playhouses than at the amphitheatres – plays regularly transferred between the two kinds of venue. There were no sets or machinery to create *illusion*, but the painted cloths behind the players would have created *spectacle*, and conventional costumes like Rafe's blue coat or the leather coat probably used to make Jasper a ghost[61] as well as stage properties, portable and nonportable, would have suggested locations.[62] The boy laments that his company cannot present 'a house covered with black velvet, and a lady in beaten gold' (IV, 42–3), but other 'houses' (or stage 'mansions'[63]) thrust out upon the stage may have been used for Rafe's shop or at least the locales associated with Venturewell, Merrythought, and Barbaroso. (A barber surgeon's pole would quickly fix the irony of that sequence.) Alternatively actors in these sequences may have come downstage from a distinctively furnished 'discovery space' behind the middle door of the tiring-house façade. It is unlikely that there were practical windows in the upper part of the

---

[59] Keith Sturgess, *Jacobean Private Theatre*, (London, 1987).

[60] Michael Hattaway, *Elizabethan Popular Theatre*, (London, 1982), pp. 72–9.

[61] Hattaway, p. 87.

[62] Alan C. Dessen, *Elizabethan Stage Conventions and Modern Interpreters*, (Cambridge, 1984), pp. 84–104.

[63] Hattaway, pp. 37–9.

façade to be used by Merrythought: when he appeared 'within' or 'aloft' he probably shared part of the music room above the stage with the playhouse musicians. There was obviously a need for at least some artificial lighting, which could, on occasion, have heightened stage effects, even creating a degree of life-likeness, but overall this was an actors' and not a scene-painters' theatre.[64]

Music was played between the acts, perhaps so that candles could be trimmed. In *The Knight* as well as music we find inserted pieces of action or 'interludes'. The one that concludes Act III consists of a jig, a probably suggestive antic dance[65] that is performed by the company and which presumably was caviar not only to the Citizen and Wife but to the more judicious spectators. (In private playhouse texts jigs are generally dismissed as representative of the kinds of inferior dramatic fare to be found in amphitheatres like the Fortune and the Red Bull.)

As with the dramatic action, the theatrical spectacle of *The Knight* probably mimicked insurrectionary games played outside the playhouse. A modern director could take hints for costuming from another description of misrule, this one from Philip Stubbes:

> First of all the wild heads of the parish conventing together, chose themselves a grand captain (of mischief) whom they ennoble with the title of my Lord of Misrule, and him they crown with great solemnity, and adopt for their king. The king anointed, chooseth forth or twenty, forty, three score or a hundred lusty guts like unto himself, to wait upon His Lordly Majesty, and to guard his noble person. Then every one of these his men he investeth with his liveries of green, yellow or some other light wanton colour. And as though that were not bawdy enough I should say, they bedeck themselves with gold rings, precious stones and other jewels. This done, they tie about either leg twenty or forty bells with rich handkerchiefs in their hands, and sometimes laid across over their shoulders and necks, borrow for the most part of their pretty Mopsies and loving Bessies, for bussying them [either 'kissing them' or 'adorning themselves'] in the dark. These things set in order, they have their hobby horses, dragons and other antics [half men, half beasts], together with their bawdy pipes and thundering drummers, to strike up the Devil's Dance withal, then march these heathen company towards the church and churchyard, their pipers piping, drummers thundering, their stumps [legs] dancing, their bells jingling, their handkerchiefs swinging about their heads like madmen, their hobby horses and other monsters skirmishing amongst the throng; and in this sort they go to the church (though the minister be at prayer or preaching) dancing and swing-

---

[64] Sturgess, p. 37.
[65] See Baskervill, pp. 145n, and 368.

ing their handkerchiefs over their heads, in the church, like devils incarnate.[66]

If the original players of Rafe, George, and Nell matched the cheerful energy of the above, their parts also demand a particular kind of playing, a Brechtian doubleness or knowingness. They act as themselves and as chorus, addressing the spectators directly and delivering both inadvertent scatological jokes – a gesture towards the stage cloth depicting the 'Confutation of Saint Paul' (Interlude II, 12–13), and theatrical in-jokes – 'You have shawms?' (Induction, 97) – that redound against the Blackfriars company. Lines like these could have been delivered with a wink to the gentlemen seated upon the stage, and their reactions must have mediated the effect of the action or, if they chose to speak up, tested the boys' skills in verbal improvisation.

After its first performances little is known about the play's afterlife in the theatre. The title page of Q2 reveals that it was acted by Queen Henrietta's Men at the Cockpit in Drury Lane in 1635, and it was performed at Court on 28 February, 1635–6, and may have been revived at the Cockpit in 1639 by the King and Queen's Young Company under William Beeston.[67] The Barbaroso episode (III, 309–466) may have been acted as a 'droll' entitled *The Encounter* during the Commonwealth period;[68] Pepys disliked the play when he saw its last act at the Theatre Royal on 7 May 1662,[69] and a prologue survives that may have been spoken by Nell Gwyn for a revival at the Theatre Royal between 1665 and 1667.[70]

The text has proved popular with amateur and university groups who started to rescue it from theatrical oblivion in performances from about 1900. Professional performances, however, are rare: Nigel Playfair, who had himself played Rafe in 1904 at the Royal Theatre in London, directed the play at the Birmingham Repertory in August 1919 with Noel Coward as Rafe.[71] A spectacular and over-busy production by Michael Bogdanov for the Royal Shakespeare Company opened on 10 April, 1981 at the Aldwych

---

[66] Philip Stubbes, *Anatomie of Abuses* (1583), ed. Frederick J. Furnivall, (London, 1879), pp. 146–7.

[67] J. Q. Adams, (ed.), *The Dramatic Records of Sir Henry Herbert, Master of the Revels, 1623–1673*, (New Haven, Conn., 1917), p. 56; Gurr, *Playing Companies*, pp. 424, 432,

[68] See J. J. Elson, (ed.), *The Wits or, Sport upon Sport* [1662], (Ithaca, N.Y., 1932).

[69] *The Diary of Samuel Pepys*, ed. Robert Latham and William Matthews, 11 vol., (London, 1970–83), III, p. 78.

[70] It is printed in 'R.B'., (ed.), *Covent Garden Drollery*, (London, 1672), pp. 78–9.

[71] J. C. Trewin, *The Birmingham Repertory Theatre 1913–1963*, (London, 1963), pp. 56–8.

Rafe (Timothy Spall) fells Barbaroso (III, 349ff.) in the
1981 Royal Shakespeare Company production (photo:
©Laurence Burns).

Theatre in London. Audiences unfamiliar with the play were astounded when the Grocer and his Wife, delighting in their tasteless opulence, clambered onto the stage. Timothy Spall, a 'depressed adolescent pseudo-sophisticate with boorish manners, loutish gait and adenoidal speech'[72] played Rafe, Margaret Courtenay Nell, Timothy Kightley George, Karl Johnson Humphrey, and John Woodvine Merrythought.

Note on the Text

The Knight of the Burning Pestle was first printed in a quarto dated 1613. It (Q1) was published by Walter Burre, and W. W. Greg showed that it was printed by Nicholas Okes. Two further quartos are dated 1635: the first of these (Q2) was also printed by Okes for a new publisher, 'I.S.' (John Spencer). It was set up from Q1 and adds an epistle, a prologue taken from Lyly's *Sapho and Phao*, as well as a *Dramatis Personae*. The second (Q3), which can be distinguished by its spelling 'Beamount' on the title page, contains many changes in spelling conventions which suggest that it was printed some years later, some time before the appearance of the second Beaumont and Fletcher folio in 1679. *The Knight* is one of the plays excluded from the folio of 1647 but it was reprinted from Q3 in the second folio (F).

Apart from some mislineation the text presents few difficulties. The literary and inaccurate stage directions of Q1 suggest that the text derives from the author's manuscript,[73] each of the early editions derives from its immediate predecessor, and no important changes occur.

This text is based upon the British Library copy (C.34.f.30) of Q1, collated with the British Library copies of Q2, Q3, and F. It incorporates the press corrections made in that edition as well as some readings from the later editions. (A variorum text with full bibliographical apparatus is provided by Cyrus Hoy in Volume I of *The Dramatic Works in the Beaumont and Fletcher Canon* edited by Fredson Bowers [Cambridge, 1966].) Like the seventeenth-century editions, the present text is divided into acts and 'interludes', but not scenes, as the action is linked together by the continuing presence on stage of the Citizen and his Wife. Their comments have been divided from the main body of the text by a double space to aid comprehension. As with all New Mermaid texts, spelling

---

[72] Stanley Wells, 'Time Warp', *TLS*, 1 May, 1981, p. 487; it was also reviewed by Robert Cushman, *The Observer*, 26 April, 1981.

[73] See W. W. Greg, *The Editorial Problem in Shakespeare*, (Oxford, 1942), pp. 36–7.

and punctuation have been modernized, abbreviations silently expanded, speech prefixes regularized, songs separated from the text and italicized, and all substantive departures from Q1 noted in the glossary. The music for the songs has not been reprinted as only a portion is extant, and many tunes associated with Merrythought's ballads are not contemporary with the play. However, references are given to reliable transcripts.

ABBREVIATIONS

Abbott	E. A. Abbott, *A Shakespearian Grammar* (London, 1878 edn.). References are to numbered paragraphs.
Baskervill	Charles Read Baskervill, *The Elizabethan Jig and Related Song Drama* (Chicago, 1929).
Bradbrook	M. C. Bradbrook, *The Growth and Structure of Elizabethan Comedy* (London, 1955).
Brand	J. Brand, *Faiths and Folklore* (an edition of *The Popular Antiquities of Great Britain*), ed. W. C. Hazlitt, 2 vols. (London, 1905).
Bronson	B. R. Bronson, *The Traditional Tunes of the Child Ballads*, 2 vols. (Princeton, 1958–62).
Chambers	E. K. Chambers, *The Elizabethan Stage*, 4 vols. (Oxford, 1923).
Chappell	William Chappell, *Old English Popular Music,* ed. H. E. Wooldridge, 2 vols. (London, 1893).
Dyce	*The Works of Beaumont and Fletcher*, ed. Alexander Dyce, 11 vols. (London, 1843–6).
ELN	*English Language Notes*
ELR	*English Literary Renaissance*
F	The second folio text of 1679.
Gurr	*The Knight of the Burning Pestle,* ed. Andrew Gurr (Edinburgh, 1968).
Harbage	Alfred Harbage, *Shakespeare and the Rival Traditions* (New York, 1952).
Hattaway	Michael Hattaway, *Elizabethan Popular Theatre* (London, 1982).
Hunter	G. K. Hunter, *English Drama 1586–1642* (Oxford, 1997).
Laroque	François Laroque, *Shakespeare's Festive World*, trans. Janet Lloyd (Cambridge, 1991).
MARDIE	*Medieval and Renaissance Drama in England*
MLN	*Modern Language Notes*
MLQ	*Modern Language Quarterly*
Murch	*The Knight of the Burning Pestle*, ed. H. S. Murch, Yale Studies in English, XXXIII (New York, 1908).
Partridge	Eric Partridge, *Shakespeare's Bawdy* (London, 1968).
Poulton	Diana Poulton, *John Dowland* (London, 1972).
PQ	*Philological Quarterly*
Q1	The first quarto of 1613.
Q1^c	Corrected copy of Q1.
Q1^u	Uncorrected copy of Q1.

Q2	The second quarto of 1635
Q3	The third quarto (falsely dated 1635).
s.d.	Stage direction
s.p.	Speech prefix
RES	*Review of English Studies*
SEL	*Studies in English Literature*
Simpson	Claude M. Simpson, *The British Broadside Ballad and its Music* (New Brunswick, 1966).
Smith	Irwin Smith, *Shakespeare's Blackfriars Playhouse* (New York, 1964).
SP	*Studies in Philology*
Stow	John Stow, *A Survey of London*, ed. C. L. Kingsford, 2 vols, (Oxford, 1908).
Stubbes	Philip Stubbes, *Anatomy of Abuses* (1583), ed. F. J. Furnivall, 2 vols, (London, 1879).
Sugden	Edward Sugden, *A Topographical Dictionary to the Works of Shakespeare and his Contemporaries* (Manchester, 1925).
Tilley	M. P. Tilley, *A Dictionary of the Proverbs in England in the Sixteenth and Seventeenth Centuries* (Ann Arbor, 1950).
TLS	*Times Literary Supplement*
Zitner	*The Knight of the Burning Pestle*, ed. Sheldon P. Zitner (Manchester, 1984).

FURTHER READING

The standard edition of Beaumont and Fletcher is *The Dramatic Works in the Beaumont and Fletcher Canon*, 10 vols. (Cambridge: Cambridge University Press, 1966–96) under the general editorship of Fredson Bowers. Modern editions of *The Knight* include those edited by R. M. Alden in the Belles-Lettres Series (Boston, 1910), Cyrus Hoy (old spelling) in Volume 1 (1966) of the Cambridge edition, John Doebler in the Regents Renaissance Drama Series (London, 1967), Andrew Gurr in the Fountainwell Drama Texts (Edinburgh, 1968), and Sheldon Zitner in the Revels Plays (Manchester, 1984).

Useful material will also be found in:

W. W. Appleton, *Beaumont and Fletcher, a Critical Study* (London: George Allen & Unwin, 1956).
Dana Aspinall, 'The Role of Folk Humor in Seventeenth-Century Receptions of Beaumont's *The Knight of the Burning Pestle*', PQ, LXXVI (1997), pp. 169–91.
Lee Bliss, *Francis Beaumont* (Boston: Twayne, 1987).
— 'Don Quixote in England: the Case for *The Knight of the Burning Pestle*', Viator, XVIII (1987), pp. 361–80.
— ' "Plot me no Plots": The Life of Drama and the Drama of Life in *The Knight of the Burning Pestle*', MLQ, XLV(1984), pp. 3–21.
Michael D. Bristol, *Carnival and Theatre* (London: Methuen, 1985).
J. F. Danby, *Poets on Fortune's Hill* (London: Faber & Faber, 1952).
Barbara Knight Degyansky, 'A Reconsideration: George and Nell of *The Knight of the Burning Pestle*', ELN, XXIII (1986), pp. 27–32.
Janette Dillon, ' "Is Not All the World Mile End, Mother?": The Blackfriars Theater, the City of London, and *The Knight of the Burning Pestle*', MARDIE, IX (1997), pp. 127–48.
J. Doebler, 'Beaumont's *The Knight of the Burning Pestle* and the Prodigal Son Plays', SEL, V (1965), pp. 333–44.
Brian Gibbons, *Jacobean City Comedy* (London: Methuen, 1968).
Andrew Gurr, *The Shakespearean Stage, 1574–1642* (Cambridge: Cambridge University Press, 1970).
— *Playgoing in Shakespeare's London* (Cambridge: Cambridge University Press, 1987).
— *The Shakespearian Playing Companies* (Oxford: Clarendon Press, 1996).

Michael Hattaway, *Elizabethan Popular Theatre* (London: Routledge, 1982).

Richard Hosley, 'A Reconstruction of the Second Blackfriars' in David Galloway, (ed.), *The Elizabethan Theatre* (London: Macmillan, 1970).

Pierre Iselin, (ed.), *F. Beaumont ... 'The Knight of the Burning Pestle'* (Paris: Didier Érudition, 1996).

Arthur C. Kirsch, *Jacobean Dramatic Perspectives* (Charlottesville: University Press of Virginia, 1972).

Clifford Leech, *The John Fletcher Plays* (London, Chatto & Windus, 1962).

E. S. Lindsey, 'The Original Music for *The Knight of the Burning Pestle*', *SP*, XXVI (1929), pp. 425–13.

Lawrence Manley, (ed.), *London in the Age of Shakespeare* (London: Croom Helm, 1986).

Ronald F. Miller, 'Dramatic Form and Dramatic Imagination in Beaumont's *The Knight of the Burning Pestle*', *ELR*, VIII (1978), pp. 67–84.

Laurie E. Osborne, 'Female Audiences and Female Authority in *The Knight of the Burning Pestle*', *Exemplaria,* III (1991), pp. 491–517.

E. C. Pettet, *Shakespeare and the Romance Tradition* (London: Staples, 1949).

Thomas Pettitt, 'Local and "Customary" Drama', in *A Companion to English Renaissance Literature and Culture*, ed. Michael Hattaway (Oxford: Blackwell, 2000), pp. 464–76.

David A. Samuelson, 'The Order in Beaumont's *Knight of the Burning Pestle*', *ELR ,* IX (1979), pp. 302–18.

Michael Shapiro, *Children of the Revels: the Boy Companies of Shakespeare's Time and their Plays* (New York: Columbia University Press, 1977).

Glenn A. Steinberg, ' "You know the plot / We both agreed on?": Plot, Self-consciousness, and *The London Merchant* in *The Knight of the Burning Pestle'*, *MARDIE,* V, (1991), pp. 211–24.

Keith Sturgess, *Jacobean Private Theatre* (London: Methuen, 1987).

Robert Weimann, *Shakespeare and the Popular Tradition in the Theater* (London: Johns Hopkins University Press, 1978).

THE
KNIGHT OF
the Burning Peſtle.

——————————— *Quod ſi*
Iudicium ſubtile, videndis artibus illud
Ad libros & ad hæc Muſarum dona vocares:
Bæotum in craſſo iurares aëre natos.
Horat. in Epiſt. ad Oct. Aug.

Aut prodeſſe ſolent aut delectare ſvita.

LONDON,
Printed for *Walter Burre*, and are to be ſold at the
ſigne of the Crane in Paules Church-yard.
1613.

[EPISTLE]

To His Many Ways Endeared
Friend, Master Robert Keysar

Sir, this unfortunate child who in eight days (as lately I have
learned) was begot and born, soon after was by his parents
(perhaps because he was so unlike his brethren) exposed to
the wide world, who for want of judgement, or not understanding the privy mark of irony about it (which showed it   5
was no offspring of any vulgar brain) utterly rejected it; so
that for want of acceptance it was even ready to give up the
ghost, and was in danger to have been smothered in perpetual oblivion, if you (out of your direct antipathy to
ingratitude) had not been moved both to relieve and cher-   10
ish it. Wherein I must needs commend both your judgement, understanding, and singular love to good wits. You
afterwards sent it to me, yet being an infant and somewhat
ragged; I have fostered it privately in my bosom these two
years, and now to show my love return it to you, clad in   15
good lasting clothes, which scarce memory will wear out,
and able to speak for itself; and, withal, as it telleth me,
desirous to try his fortune in the world, where if yet it be
welcome, father, foster-father, nurse, and child, all have
their desired end. If it be slighted or traduced, it hopes his   20
father will beget him a younger brother who shall revenge
his quarrel, and challenge the world either of fond and
merely literal interpretation, or illiterate misprision.

Robert Keysar a wealthy London goldsmith who had financed the Children of
the Revels at the Blackfriars Theatre from about 1606 (see Smith, pp. 193 ff.)

2 *his parents* Would suggest joint authorship were it not for 'father' in l. 19.

3 *his brethren* other plays currently being produced

6 *no offspring of any vulgar brain* not an ordinary citizen comedy
rejected it Either the author did not get his play performed or it was not well
received.

13–14 *somewhat ragged* the author's foul papers, or, possibly, unrevised

19 *father ... child* author, dedicatee, publisher, and play
child, all Q1ᶜ (child, Q1ᵘ)

21 *younger brother* another play

22–3 *fond and merely* foolish and completely

3

Perhaps it will be thought to be of the race of *Don Quixote*:
we both may confidently swear it is his elder above a year;   25
and therefore may (by virtue of his birthright) challenge the
wall of him. I doubt not but they will meet in their adventures, and I hope the breaking of one staff will make them
friends; and perhaps they will combine themselves, and
travel through the world to seek their adventures. So I   30
commit him to his good fortune, and myself to your love.

Your assured friend
W.B.

---

24 *Don Quixote* Shelton's translation of Cervantes' parody was published in 1612,
   but both the translation and the original (1605) had circulated before then.
26–7 *challenge the wall of him* demand the safest part of the footpath, hence
   claim precedence
28 *breaking of one staff* possibly the barber's pole (see III, 333 s.d.) – an incident
   borrowed from Cervantes
33 *W.B.* Walter Burre, the play's publisher

To the Readers of this Comedy

Gentlemen, the world is so nice in these our times, that for
apparel, there is no fashion; for music, which is a rare art
(though now slighted), no instrument; for diet, none but the
French kickshaws that are delicate; and for plays, no invention but that which now runneth an invective way, touch-   5
ing some particular person, or else it is condemned before
it is throughly understood. This is all that I have to say, that
the author had no intent to wrong anyone in this comedy,
but as a merry passage, here and there interlaced it with
delight, which he hopes will please all, and be hurtful to   10
none.

To The Readers from Q2 (om. Q1)

  1 *nice* fastidious
  4 *kickshaws* <French *quelque chose,* insubstantial dainties
  6 *condemned* disdained
  7 *throughly* thoroughly

THE PROLOGUE

Where the bee can suck no honey, she leaves her sting behind; and where the bear cannot find origanum to heal his grief, he blasteth all other leaves with his breath. We fear it is like to fare so with us, that seeing you cannot draw from our labours sweet content, you leave behind you a 5 sour mislike and with open reproach blame our good meaning because you cannot reap the wonted mirth. Our intent was at this time to move inward delight, not outward lightness; and to breed (if it might be) soft smiling, not loud laughing, knowing it to the wise to be as great pleasure to 10 hear counsel mixed with wit, as to the foolish to have sport mingled with rudeness. They were banished the theatre of Athens, and from Rome hissed, that brought parasites on the stage with apish actions, or fools with uncivil habits, or courtesans with immodest words. We have endeavoured to 15 be as far from unseemly speeches to make your ears glow, as we hope you will be free from unkind reports, or, mistaking the author's intention (who never aimed at any one particular in this play), to make our cheeks blush. And thus I leave it and thee to thine own censure, to like, or dislike. 20 *Vale.*

Prologue from Q2, where it is reprinted from Lyly's *Sappho and Phao* (1584), (om. Q1)
  2 *origanum* herb from marjoram family
 10 *as great* ed. (a great Q2)
 13 *parasites* 'men that frequent rich tables and obtain their welcome by flattery' (Johnson)
 21 *Vale* Farewell

THE SPEAKERS' NAMES

The Prologue
Then a Citizen
The Citizen's Wife, and
Rafe, her man, sitting below amidst the spectators
[Venturewell], a rich merchant   5
Jasper, his apprentice
Master Humphrey, a friend to the merchant
Luce, the merchant's daughter
Mistress Merrythought, Jasper's mother
Michael, a second son of Mistress Merrythought   10
Old Master Merrythought
[Tim,] a squire ⎱
[George,] a dwarf ⎰ [Apprentices]
A Tapster
A Boy that danceth and singeth   15
An Host
A Barber
[Three Captive] Knights
[A Captive Woman]
A Sergeant   20
Soldiers
[Boys
William Hamerton, a pewterer
George Greengoose, a poulterer
Pompiona, daughter to the King of Moldavia]   25

The Speakers' Names from Q2 (om. Q1)

  8 *the* F (om. Q2)

 18 *[Three Captive] Knights* ed. (Two Knights Q2)

 18–20 Q2–3, F list *A Captaine* between *Knights* and *A Sergeant*; this must refer to
     Rafe in the Mile End scene (V, 89 ff.)

THE FAMOUS HISTORY OF THE KNIGHT
OF THE BURNING PESTLE

[Induction

GENTLEMEN *seated upon the stage. The* CITIZEN, *his*
WIFE, *and* RAFE *below among the audience*]

Enter PROLOGUE

[PROLOGUE]
From all that's near the court, from all that's great
Within the compass of the city-walls,
We now have brought our scene –

Enter CITIZEN [*from audience below*]

CITIZEN
Hold your peace, goodman boy.
PROLOGUE
What do you mean, sir? 5
CITIZEN
That you have no good meaning. This seven years there
hath been plays at this house, I have observed it, you have
still girds at citizens; and now you call your play *The
London Merchant*. Down with your title, boy, down with
your title! 10
PROLOGUE
Are you a member of the noble city?

---

0 s.d.1 GENTLEMEN The behaviour of the tobacco smoking gallants who paid for
stools on the stage itself is satirised in Beaumont's *The Woman Hater* (1606) I.iii,
Dekker's *The Gull's Hornbook* (1609) Ch. iii, and in plays by Jonson.

0 s.d.3 PROLOGUE wore a long black velvet cloak and a garland of bays

1 *great* Q1 (great, *conj. this edn*)

6–7 *seven ... house* The Children of the Revels played at Blackfriars from 1600 to
1608.

8 *still* always
   girds sneers

8–9 *The London Merchant* possibly a lost play by Ford, but more probably the
name of the play dealing with Venturewell and his family

10 *title* A placard bearing the name of the play may have hung on the stage.

11 *member* inhabitant

9

CITIZEN
  I am.
PROLOGUE
  And a freeman?
CITIZEN
  Yea, and a grocer. → technically a merchant?
PROLOGUE
  So, grocer, then by your sweet favour, we intend no abuse   15
  to the city.
CITIZEN
  No, sir? Yes, sir! If you were not resolved to play the jacks,
  what need you study for new subjects, purposely to abuse
  your betters? Why could not you be contented, as well as
  others, with *The Legend of Whittington*, or *The Life and*   20
  Death of Sir Thomas Gresham, with the Building of the
  Royal Exchange, or *The Story of Queen Elenor, with the*
  Rearing of London Bridge upon Woolsacks?
PROLOGUE
  You seem to be an understanding man. What would you
  have us do, sir?   25
CITIZEN
  Why, present something notably in honour of the commons
  of the city.

---

13 *freeman* enjoying the privileges of the City; admission to the rank came after
   serving a term of apprenticeship
14 *grocer* a member of one of the most important of the twelve great livery
   companies of London
15 *favour* pun on favour as 'face'
17 *play the jacks* play the knave, do a mean trick (Tilley J8)
20 ff. Plays from public theatres that glorified the City: Dick Whittington was the
   legendary Lord Mayor who rose from low estate to great fortune (a play about
   him was entered on the Stationers' Register in 1605); Sir Thomas Gresham
   appears in Heywood's *2 If You Know Not Me* (1605); he had built the Royal
   Exchange, a cosmopolitan place of resort that was destroyed in the fire of 1666;
   Queen Elenor is probably from Peele's *Edward I* printed in 1593; 'The Building
   of London Bridge upon Wool Packs' was the name of a dance that got its name
   from a levy upon wool raised to pay for the bridge.
24 *understanding* a pun, since the spectators were below the stage; cf. Jonson,
   Bartholomew Fair, Induction, 'the understanding gentlemen o' the ground'
26 *commons* the body of freemen; for texts that exalted London's citizenry, see
   Lawrence Manley, (ed.), 'Worthies Remembered', *London in the Age of*
   Shakespeare, (London, 1986), pp. 209–37

PROLOGUE
Why, what do you say to *The Life and Death of Fat Drake,
or the Repairing of Fleet-privies*?

CITIZEN
I do not like that; but I will have a citizen, and he shall be   30
of my own trade.

PROLOGUE
Oh, you should have told us your mind a month since. Our
play is ready to begin now.

CITIZEN
'Tis all one for that; I will have a grocer, and he shall do
admirable things.   35

PROLOGUE
What will you have him do?

CITIZEN
Marry, I will have him –

WIFE below

WIFE
Husband, husband!   → *interjects, excited*

RAFE below

RAFE
Peace, mistress.

WIFE
Hold thy peace, Rafe; I know what I do, I warrant'ee. –   40
Husband, husband.

CITIZEN
What say'st thou, cony?   *term of endearment*

WIFE
Let him kill a lion with a pestle, husband; let him kill a lion
with a pestle.

*grocer's typical
tool of trade;
blunt, phallic joke*

28 *Fat Drake* probably a sarcastic invention of the Prologue

29 *Fleet-privies* Fleet Ditch served as a sewer

32–3 *Our play is ready to begin now.* The players were in fact accustomed to
demands for a change in the programme; see Bradbrook, pp. 24–5.

35 *admirable* wonderful

42 *cony* rabbit, term of endearment; cf. Chapman, *The Blind Beggar of Alexandria*
(1595), V.37–9:

New-fashion terms I like not, for a man
To call his wife 'cony', forsooth, and 'lamb':
And 'pork' and 'mutton', he as well may say.

Like all words containing 'con', it had sexual connotations.

CITIZEN

    So he shall. – I'll have him kill a lion with a pestle.   45

WIFE

    Husband, shall I come up, husband?

CITIZEN

    Ay, cony. – Rafe, help your mistress this way. – Pray,
gentlemen, make her a little room. – I pray you, sir, lend me
your hand to help up my wife; I thank you, sir. – So.

She interjects herself physically

[WIFE *comes up onto stage*]

WIFE

    By your leave, gentlemen all, I'm something troublesome;   50
I'm a stranger here; I was ne'er at one of these plays, as they
say, before; but I should have seen *Jane Shore* once, and my
husband hath promised me any time this twelvemonth to
carry me to *The Bold Beauchamps*; but in truth he did not.
I pray you bear with me.   55

CITIZEN

    Boy, let my wife and I have a couple of stools, and then
begin, and let the grocer do rare things.

PROLOGUE

    But sir, we have never a boy to play him; everyone hath a
part already.

WIFE

    Husband, husband, for God's sake let Rafe play him;   60
beshrew me if I do not think he will go beyond them all.

CITIZEN

    Well remembered, wife. – Come up, Rafe. – I'll tell you,
gentlemen, let them but lend him a suit of reparel and
necessaries, and, by gad, if any of them all blow wind in the
tail on him, I'll be hanged. *→ protective?*   65

---

45 *kill a lion with a pestle* Battles with wild beasts were common in the romances,
    and one of the prentices in Heywood's *The Four Prentices of London* (1594)
    claims to have killed a lion single-handed.

46 *shall I come up* For a woman to sit on the stage was both unusual and immod-
    est.

52 *Jane Shore* Also a citizen's wife and mistress of Edward IV, she appears in
    Heywood's *Edward IV* printed in 1600; there are references in Henslowe's *Diary*
    to plays about her composed by Chettle and Day.

54 *The Bold Beauchamps* a lost play ascribed to Heywood

56 *of* Q2 (om. Q1)

61 *beshrew me* the devil take me

63 *reparel* archaic synonym for apparel

64–5 *blow wind in the tail on* come near (from horse-racing)

[RAFE *comes up onto stage*]

WIFE

I pray you, youth, let him have a suit of reparel. – I'll be
sworn, gentlemen, my husband tells you true: he will act
you sometimes at our house, that all the neighbours cry
on him. He will fetch you up a couraging part so in the
garret that we are all as feared, I warrant you, that we   70
quake again. We'll fear our children with him: if they be
never so unruly, do but cry, 'Rafe comes, Rafe comes', to
them, and they'll be as quiet as lambs. – Hold up thy head,
Rafe; show the gentlemen what thou canst do; speak a
huffing part; I warrant you the gentlemen will accept of it.   75

CITIZEN

Do, Rafe, do.

RAFE

By heaven, methinks it were an easy leap
To pluck bright honour from the pale-faced moon,
Or dive into the bottom of the sea,
Where never fathom line touched any ground,   80
And pluck up drowned honour from the lake of hell.

quote from IV Henry

CITIZEN

How say you, gentlemen, is it not as I told you?

WIFE

Nay, gentlemen, he hath played before, my husband says,
Mucedorus before the wardens of our company.

CITIZEN

Ay, and he should have played Jeronimo with a shoemaker   85
for a wager.

PROLOGUE

He shall have a suit of apparel if he will go in.

68–9 *cry out on* complain of

69 *couraging* spirited

75 *huffing* puffed up, bombastic

77 ff. *By heaven ... lake of hell* Hotspur's speech in *1 Henry IV*, I.iii.201 ff., a fine
bombastic or 'huffing' part; Rafe substitutes a commonplace 'from the lake of
hell' for Shakespeare's 'by the locks'.

84 *Mucedorus* the hero of a very popular and absurdly extravagant play, first
printed anonymously in 1598, in which scenes of romantic adventure are laced
with buffoonery
before the wardens Performances by livery companies in the guild halls and at
court (cf. *A Midsummer Night's Dream*) continued throughout the first half of
the seventeenth century.

85 *Jeronimo* (Hieronimo), hero of Kyd's *The Spanish Tragedy*

87 *go in* to the tiring-house behind the stage

CITIZEN

In, Rafe; in, Rafe; and set out the grocery in their kind, if
thou lov'st me.

[*Exit* RAFE]

WIFE

I warrant our Rafe will look finely when he's dressed.   90

PROLOGUE

But what will you have it called?

CITIZEN

The Grocer's Honour.   ↗ OED

PROLOGUE

Methinks *The Knight of the Burning Pestle* were better.

WIFE

I'll be sworn, husband, that's as good a name as can be.

CITIZEN

Let it be so. Begin, begin; my wife and I will sit down.   95

PROLOGUE

I pray you, do.

CITIZEN

What stately music have you? You have shawms?

PROLOGUE

Shawms? No.

CITIZEN

No? I'm a thief if my mind did not give me so. Rafe plays a
stately part, and he must needs have shawms; I'll be at the   100
charge of them myself, rather than we'll be without them.

PROLOGUE

So you are like to be.

CITIZEN

Why, and so I will be. There's two shillings; let's have the
waits of Southwark. They are as rare fellows as any are in
England; and that will fetch them all o'er the water with a   105
vengeance, as if they were mad.

PROLOGUE

You shall have them. Will you sit down then?

---

88 *in their kind* fittingly: each company had a distinctive livery
93 *The Knight of the Burning Pestle* see Introduction, p. xiv
    Burning Gilded (see II, 298)
97 *shawms* forerunners of oboes
104 *waits* band of wind-instrument players maintained by the City at public expense
105 *o'er the water* The Borough of Southwark is across the river from the City where
    the theatre was; 'two shillings would have been a fair day's wage, though not
    enough to make them enthusiastic' (Gurr).

CITIZEN
  Ay. – Come, wife.
WIFE
  Sit you merry all, gentlemen. I'm bold to sit amongst you
  for my ease.   110
PROLOGUE
  From all that's near the court, from all that's great
  Within the compass of the city-walls,
  We now have brought our scene. Fly far from hence
  All private taxes, immodest phrases,
  Whate'er may but show like vicious: 115
  For wicked mirth never true pleasure brings,
  But honest minds are pleased with honest things. –
  Thus much for that we do; but for Rafe's part you must
  answer for yourself.   [*Exit*]
CITIZEN
  Take you no care for Rafe; he'll discharge himself, I 120
  warrant you.
WIFE
  I'faith, gentlemen, I'll give my word for Rafe.

Act I

Enter MERCHANT [VENTUREWELL] *and* JASPER, *his
prentice*

MERCHANT
  Sirrah, I'll make you know you are my prentice,
  And whom my charitable love redeemed
  Even from the fall of fortune; gave thee heat
  And growth to be what now thou art, new cast thee;

114 *private taxes* Possibly a reference to the personal satires used as weapons in the
    War of the Theatres (see Bradbrook, pp. 103 ff. and Harbage, pp. 90 ff., but see
    Hunter, pp. 283 ff.); like Jonson, Beaumont thought that the satiric function of
    drama was to correct general folly and vice and not particular persons; cf. the
    prologue to *The Woman Hater*.
    immodest phrases Marston's plays for boys were laced with obscenities.
118–19 *you ... yourself* printed as verse in Q1
120 *discharge himself* acquit himself, also ejaculate (Partridge, p. 94)

Act I ed. Actus primi, Scoena prima Q1
  1 *Sirrah* used to address an inferior
  3–4 *heat / And growth* shelter and sustenance
  4 *new cast thee* formed you again

Adding the trust of all I have at home,   5
In foreign staples, or upon the sea,
To thy direction; tied the good opinions
Both of myself and friends to thy endeavours:
So fair were thy beginnings. But with these,
As I remember, you had never charge   10
To love your master's daughter, and even then
When I had found a wealthy husband for her.
I take it, sir, you had not; but, however,
I'll break the neck of that commission
And make you know you are but a merchant's factor.   15

JASPER
Sir, I do liberally confess I am yours,
Bound both by love and duty to your service,
In which my labour hath been all my profit.
I have not lost in bargain, nor delighted
To wear your honest gains upon my back,   20
Nor have I given a pension to my blood,
Or lavishly in play consumed your stock.
These, and the miseries that do attend them,
I dare with innocence proclaim are strangers
To all my temperate actions. For your daughter,   25
If there be any love to my deservings
Borne by her virtuous self, I cannot stop it;
Nor am I able to refrain her wishes.
She's private to herself and best of knowledge
Whom she'll make so happy as to sigh for.   30
Besides, I cannot think you mean to match her
Unto a fellow of so lame a presence,
One that hath little left of nature in him.

MERCHANT
'Tis very well, sir. I can tell your wisdom
How all this shall be cured.

JASPER   Your care becomes you.   35

MERCHANT
And thus it must be, sir: I here discharge you

---

6 *staples* centres of commerce, or storehouses
11 *even* especially
13 *however* notwithstanding [my trust in you]
14 *commission* delegated authority
15 *factor* deputy (who buys and sells for his master)
21 *pension to my blood* licence (income) to my passion
22 *play* gambling
28 *refrain* curb
29 *private … knowledge* free to decide and knows best

My house and service. Take your liberty,
And when I want a son I'll send for you.   *Exit*

JASPER
These be the fair rewards of them that love.
Oh you that live in freedom, never prove   40
The travail of a mind led by desire!

Enter LUCE

LUCE
Why, how now, friend? Struck with my father's thunder?
JASPER
Struck, and struck dead, unless the remedy
Be full of speed and virtue. I am now
What I expected long, no more your father's.   45
LUCE
But mine.
JASPER   But yours, and only yours, I am;
That's all I have to keep me from the statute.
You dare be constant still?
LUCE   Oh, fear me not.
In this I dare be better than a woman:
Nor shall his anger nor his offers move me,   50
Were they both equal to a prince's power.
JASPER
You know my rival?
LUCE   Yes, and love him dearly,
Even as I love an ague or foul weather;
I prithee, Jasper, fear him not.
JASPER   Oh, no,
I do not mean to do him so much kindness.   55
But to our own desires: you know the plot
We both agreed on?
LUCE   Yes, and will perform
My part exactly.

40 *prove* experience
41 *travail* suffering
42 *friend* dearest, my love
44 *speed and virtue* goodness and power
47 *the statute* either that against 'Rogues, vagabonds, and sturdy beggars' (39 Eliz. Ch. 4), or the 'Statute of Apprentices' (5 Eliz. Ch. 4, ix–x), passed in 1562, which required all young persons to be apprenticed and any that departed from their master's parish without a testimonial to be imprisoned
49 *I ... woman* I shall eschew the habitual inconstancy of my sex

JASPER   I desire no more.
 Farewell, and keep my heart; 'tis yours.
LUCE   I take it;
 He must do miracles makes me forsake it.   60

Exeunt

CITIZEN
 Fie upon 'em, little infidels: what a matter's here now! Well,
 I'll be hanged for a halfpenny if there be not some
 abomination knavery in this play. Well, let 'em look to't.
 Rafe must come, and if there be any tricks a-brewing –
WIFE
 Let 'em brew and bake too, husband, a God's name. Rafe   65
 will find all out, I warrant you, and they were older than
 they are. –

[Enter BOY]

 I pray, my pretty youth, is Rafe ready?
BOY
 He will be presently.
WIFE
 Now, I pray you, make my commendations unto him, and   70
 withal carry him this stick of liquorice. Tell him his mistress
 sent it him, and bid him bite a piece; 'twill open his pipes
 the better, say.

[Exit BOY]

Enter MERCHANT *and* MASTER HUMPHREY

MERCHANT
 Come, sir, she's yours; upon my faith, she's yours;
 You have my hand. For other idle lets   75
 Between your hopes and her, thus with a wind
 They are scattered and no more. My wanton prentice,
 That like a bladder blew himself with love,
 I have let out, and sent him to discover
 New masters yet unknown.

66 *and* if
68 *pretty* clever, fine
72 *open his pipes* Liquorice was used for loosening phlegm and clearing the voice
 (Murch); the Wife is free with medical advice since her grocer husband would
 have sold drugs.
75 *idle lets* foolish obstacles

HUMPHREY   I thank you, sir,   80
  Indeed, I thank you, sir; and ere I stir
  It shall be known, however you do deem,
  I am of gentle blood and gentle seem.
MERCHANT
  Oh, sir, I know it certain.
HUMPHREY   Sir, my friend,
  Although, as writers say, all things have end,   85
  And that we call a pudding hath his two,
  Oh, let it not seem strange, I pray, to you,
  If in this bloody simile I put
  My love, more endless than frail things or gut.

WIFE
  Husband, I prithee, sweet lamb, tell me one thing, but tell   90
  me truly: – stay, youths, I beseech you, till I question my
  husband.
CITIZEN
  What is it, mouse?
WIFE
  Sirrah, didst thou ever see a prettier child? How it behaves
  itself, I warrant ye, and speaks, and looks, and perts up the   95
  head? – I pray you, brother, with your favour, were you
  never none of Master Monkester's scholars?
CITIZEN
  Chicken, I prithee heartily, contain thyself; the childer are
  pretty childer; but when Rafe comes, lamb –
WIFE
  Ay, when Rafe comes, cony. – Well, my youth, you may   100
  proceed.

MERCHANT
  Well, sir, you know my love, and rest, I hope,
  Assured of my consent. Get but my daughter's,

85–6 Compare the proverb 'Everything has an end and a pudding has two' (Tilley
    E121).
86 *pudding* blood sausage, entrails
94 *prettier* cleverer, better trained
95 *perts* perks
97 *Monkester* Richard Mulcaster had been Master of the Merchant Taylors' school
    in the 1570s, and became High Master of Paul's School in 1596 'where he taught
    Nathan Field, the Blackfriars Boys' best player, who played the lead in *The
    Knight*' (Andrew Gurr, *The Shakespearian Playing Companies,* (Oxford, 1996),
    p. 219).
98 *childer* dialect form of 'children'

And wed her when you please. You must be bold,
And clap in close unto her. Come, I know   105
You have language good enough to win a wench.

WIFE
A whoreson tyrant! H'as been an old stringer in's days, I
warrant him.

HUMPHREY
I take your gentle offer, and withal
Yield love again for love reciprocal.   110
MERCHANT
What, Luce! Within there!

Enter LUCE

LUCE   Called you, sir?
MERCHANT   I did.
Give entertainment to this gentleman
And see you be not froward. – To her, sir;
My presence will but be an eyesore to you.   *Exit*
HUMPHREY
Fair Mistress Luce, how do you? Are you well?   115
Give me your hand, and then I pray you tell
How doth your little sister and your brother,
And whether you love me or any other.
LUCE
Sir, these are quickly answered.
HUMPHREY   So they are,
Where women are not cruel. But how far   120
Is it now distant from this place we are in,
Unto that blessed place, your father's warren?
LUCE
What makes you think of that, sir?
HUMPHREY   Even that face;
For, stealing rabbits whilom in that place,
God Cupid, or the keeper, I know not whether,   125
Unto my cost and charges brought you thither,
And there began –

---

105 *clap* press
107 *stringer* fornicator
112 *entertainment* welcome
115–18 These lines parody the ballad or jig 'The Merry Wooing of Robin and Joan'
     (see Baskervill, pp. 195–6, 418).
122 *warren* land for breeding game
125 *whether* which

LUCE   Your game, sir.
HUMPHREY   Let no game,
  Or any thing that tendeth to the same,
  Be evermore remembered, thou fair killer,
  For whom I sat me down and brake my tiller.   130

WIFE
  There's a kind gentleman, I warrant you. When will you do
  as much for me, George?
LUCE
  Beshrew me, sir, I am sorry for your losses;
  But as the proverb says, I cannot cry.
  I would you had not seen me.
HUMPHREY   So would I,   135
  Unless you had more maw to do me good.
LUCE
  Why, cannot this strange passion be withstood?
  Send for a constable and raise the town.
HUMPHREY
  Oh no, my valiant love will batter down
  Millions of constables, and put to flight   140
  Even that great watch of Midsummer day at night.
LUCE
  Beshrew me, sir, 'twere good I yielded then;
  Weak women cannot hope, where valiant men
  Have no resistance.
HUMPHREY   Yield then; I am full
  Of pity, though I say it, and can pull   145
  Out of my pocket, thus, a pair of gloves.
  Look, Lucy, look: the dog's tooth nor the dove's
  Are not so white as these; and sweet they be,
  And whipped about with silk, as you may see.
  If you desire the price, shoot from your eye   150

130 *tiller* the beam of a crossbow, a sexual quibble
134 *proverb* 'I am sorry for thee but I cannot cry' (Tilley C872)
136 *maw* stomach, craving
141 *that great watch* An elaborate and popular pageant at which the City and
    companies mustered the militia and constables to serve for the ensuing year; see
    Stow, i. 101–3.
146 *gloves* were customarily presented as love-tokens at betrothals and weddings; see
    Brand, i. 277
150 *shoot* ed. (sure Q1)
150–1 *shoot … place* It was thought that beams emitted by the eyes were the source
    of vision.

A beam to this place, and you shall espy
'F.S.', which is to say, my sweetest honey,
They cost me three and two pence, or no money.
LUCE
  Well, sir, I take them kindly, and I thank you.
  What would you more?
HUMPHREY   Nothing.
LUCE   Why then, farewell.   155
HUMPHREY
  Nor so, nor so; for, lady, I must tell,
  Before we part, for what we met together;
  God grant me time, and patience, and fair weather.
LUCE
  Speak, and declare your mind in terms so brief.
HUMPHREY
  I shall. Then, first and foremost, for relief   160
  I call to you, if that you can afford it;
  I care not at what price, for, on my word, it
  Shall be repaid again, although it cost me
  More than I'll speak of now. For love hath tossed me
  In furious blanket like a tennis-ball,   165
  And now I rise aloft, and now I fall.
LUCE
  Alas, good gentleman, alas the day.
HUMPHREY
  I thank you heartily, and, as I say,
  Thus do I still continue without rest,
  I'th'morning like a man, at night a beast,   170
  Roaring and bellowing mine own disquiet,
  That much I fear, forsaking of my diet
  Will bring me presently to that quandàry,
  I shall bid all adieu.
LUCE   Now, by Saint Mary,
  That were great pity.
HUMPHREY   So it were, beshrew me.   175
  Then ease me, lusty Luce, and pity show me.

152 *F.S.* Perhaps a dealer's mark for the price (see R. Withington, ' "F.S., which is to
    say ..." ', *SP*, XXII [1925], 226–33), or else short for 'fine silk' – or possibly
    Humphrey bought the gloves for someone else!
153 *three and two pence* The gloves were expensive.
159 *so brief* as fair weather
161 *you, if* Q2 you, I if (Q1)
172 *diet* way of life
173 *quandàry* original stressing was quandàry
176 *lusty* pretty

LUCE

   Why, sir, you know my will is nothing worth
   Without my father's grant; get his consent,
   And then you may with assurance try me.

HUMPHREY

   The worshipful your sire will not deny me;   180
   For I have asked him, and he hath replied,
   'Sweet Master Humphrey, Luce shall be thy bride'.

LUCE

   Sweet Master Humphrey, then I am content.

HUMPHREY

   And so am I, in truth.

LUCE   Yet take me with you;
   There is another clause must be annexed,   185
   And this it is: I swore and will perform it,
   No man shall ever joy me as his wife
   But he that stole me hence. If you dare venture,
   I am yours – you need not fear, my father loves you –
   If not, farewell for ever.

HUMPHREY   Stay, nymph, stay;   190
   I have a double gelding, coloured bay,
   Sprung by his father from Barbarian kind;
   Another for myself, though somewhat blind,
   Yet true as trusty tree.

LUCE   I am satisfied;
   And so I give my hand. Our course must lie   195
   Through Waltham Forest, where I have a friend
   Will entertain us. So, farewell, Sir Humphrey,
   And think upon your business.   *Exit* LUCE

HUMPHREY   Though I die,
   I am resolved to venture life and limb
   For one so young, so fair, so kind, so trim.   200
                                Exit HUMPHREY

WIFE

   By my faith and troth, George, and, as I am virtuous, it is
   e'en the kindest young man that ever trod on shoe leather.

184 *take me with you* let this be clear
191 *double gelding* horse for two
192 *Barbarian* from the Saracen countries of North Africa (<Berber), famous for
    their breeds of horses
196 *Waltham Forest* Waltham Cross is in Hertfordshire, 12 miles N. of London; part
    of the great forest survives at Epping.

Well, go thy ways; if thou hast her not, 'tis not thy fault,
'faith.

CITIZEN

I prithee, mouse, be patient: 'a shall have her, or I'll make   205
some of 'em smoke for't.

WIFE

That's my good lamb, George. Fie, this stinking tobacco
kills me; would there were none in England. – Now I pray,
gentlemen, what good does this stinking tobacco do you?
Nothing, I warrant you; make chimneys o'your faces. – Oh,   210
husband, husband, now, now, there's Rafe, there's Rafe.

Enter RAFE *like a grocer in's shop, with two prentices*
[TIM *and* GEORGE] *reading* Palmerin of England

CITIZEN

Peace, fool, let Rafe alone. – Hark you, Rafe; do not strain
yourself too much at the first. – Peace! – Begin, Rafe.

RAFE [*reads*]

'Then Palmerin and Trineus, snatching their lances from
their dwarfs, and clasping their helmets, galloped amain   215
after the giant; and Palmerin, having gotten a sight of him,
came posting amain, saying: "Stay, traitorous thief, for
thou mayst not so carry away her that is worth the greatest
lord in the world"; and with these words gave him a blow
on the shoulder, that he struck him besides his elephant; and   220
Trineus, coming to the knight that had Agricola behind

---

206 *of* Q2 (om. Q1)
    smoke suffer
207 *tobacco* After Sir Walter Ralegh had made smoking fashionable among gallants,
    the habit provoked many attacks including *The Metamorphosis of Tobacco*
    (1602), a poem by Beaumont's brother John, and James I's *A Counterblast to*
    Tobacco (1604).
208 *me* ed. (men Q1–3, F)
211 s.d. 1 *like a grocer in's shop* Rafe is wearing the blue of a serving-man, not the
    livery ordered by the Citizen.
211 s.d. 2 *Palmerin of England* In fact Rafe reads out of *Palmerin d'Oliva*, I. li, to
    which *Palmerin of England* was a sequel; both had been translated into English
    by Antony Munday.
212 *fool* a term of endearment
220 *elephant* The original has 'horse', but the exaggeration is intentional.
221 *Agricola* The princess Palmerin is rescuing is in the original 'Agriola': the mis-
    take may be either authorial or compositorial (see R. Proudfoot, *The Library*,
    6th Series, 4 (1982), 47–9).

burnt my tongue imagining you

him, set him soon besides his horse, with his neck broken
in the fall, so that the princess, getting out of the throng,
between joy and grief said: "All happy knight, the mirror of
all such as follow arms, now may I be well assured of the   225
love thou bearest me".' I wonder why the kings do not raise
an army of fourteen or fifteen hundred thousand men, as
big as the army that the Prince of Portigo brought against
Rosicleer, and destroy these giants; they do much hurt to
wandering damsels that go in quest of their knights.   230

WIFE
Faith, husband, and Rafe says true; for they say the King of
Portugal cannot sit at his meat, but the giants and the ettins
will come and snatch it from him.

CITIZEN
Hold thy tongue. – On, Rafe.

RAFE
And certainly those knights are much to be commended   235
who, neglecting their possessions, wander with a squire and
a dwarf through the deserts to relieve poor ladies.

WIFE
Ay, by my faith, are they, Rafe; let 'em say what they will,
they are indeed. Our knights neglect their possessions well
enough, but they do not the rest.   240

RAFE
There are no such courteous and fair well-spoken knights   *No manners*
in this age: they will call one 'the son of a whore' that   *nowadays*
Palmerin of England would have called 'fair sir'; and one
that Rosicleer would have called 'right beauteous damsel',
they will call 'damned bitch'.   245

222 *set ... horse* unhorsed him
224 *mirror* paragon
228 *Portigo* Portugal
229 *Rosicleer* Hero of Ortuñez de Calahorra's *Espejo de Principes y Caualleros*, one
    of the romances owned by Don Quixote, translated into English by Margaret
    Tyler and others as *The Mirror of ... Knighthood* (1578–1601).
232 *ettins* giants from Germanic folklore
236 *possessions* property, estates
240 *do not the rest* continue to pursue women

WIFE

I'll be sworn will they, Rafe; they have called me so an hundred times about a scurvy pipe of tobacco.

[margin handwritten: which she asked about earlier]

RAFE

But what brave spirit could be content to sit in his shop with a flappet of wood and a blue apron before him, selling mithridatum and dragon's water to visited houses, that might pursue feats of arms, and through his noble achievements procure such a famous history to be written of his heroic prowess?   250

[margin handwritten: why be a shopkeeper when there's glory to be had?]

CITIZEN

Well said, Rafe, some more of those words, Rafe.

WIFE

They go finely, by my troth.   255

RAFE

Why should not I then pursue this course, both for the credit of myself and our company? For amongst all the worthy books of achievements I do not call to mind that I yet read of a grocer errant. I will be the said knight. Have you heard of any that hath wandered unfurnished of his squire and dwarf? My elder prentice Tim shall be my trusty squire, and little George my dwarf. Hence my blue apron! Yet in remembrance of my former trade, upon my shield shall be portrayed a burning pestle, and I will be called the Knight o'th' Burning Pestle.   260

                                                                          265

WIFE

Nay, I dare swear thou wilt not forget thy old trade; thou wert ever meek.

RAFE

Tim.

---

249 *flappet* small flap (of the counter or the shop's shutter)

250 *mithridatum* herbal medicine named after King Mithridates, used against poison and disease

dragon's water used against fevers and the plague

visited by plague

258 For specific similarities between Rafe's adventures and the romances see Murch's notes *passim*.

259 *grocer errant* in fact 'Eustace, in Heywood's *Four Prentices of London* was a grocer's boy turned knight errant' (Zitner)

TIM

Anon.

RAFE

My beloved squire, and George my dwarf, I charge you that   270
from henceforth you never call me by any other name but
the 'Right Courteous and Valiant Knight of the Burning
Pestle', and that you never call any female by the name of a
woman or wench, but 'Fair Lady', if she have her desires, if
not, 'Distressed Damsel'; that you call all forests and heaths   275
'deserts', and all horses 'palfreys'.

WIFE

This is very fine, faith. Do the gentlemen like Rafe, think
you, husband?

CITIZEN

Ay, I warrant thee, the players would give all the shoes in
their shop for him.   280

RAFE

My beloved squire Tim, stand out. Admit this were a
desert, and over it a knight errant pricking, and I should bid
you inquire of his intents, what would you say?

TIM

Sir, my master sent me to know whither you are riding.

RAFE

No, thus: 'Fair sir, the Right Courteous and Valiant Knight   285
of the Burning Pestle commanded me to inquire upon what
adventure you are bound, whether to relieve some distressed damsels, or otherwise'.

CITIZEN

Whoreson blockhead cannot remember!

WIFE

I'faith, and Rafe told him on't before; all the gentlemen   290
heard him. – Did he not, gentlemen? Did not Rafe tell him
on't?

GEORGE

Right Courteous and Valiant Knight of the Burning Pestle,

279–80 *shoes in their shop* actors' costumes at this time were elaborate and costly
(see Hattaway, pp. 86–8).

282 *pricking* spurring, riding (see *The Faerie Queene*, I.i.1); Chaucer too rang the
changes on this word throughout his parody *Sir Thopas*.

284 *you* Q2 (your Q1)

287 *you* Q2 (your Q1)

here is a distressed damsel, to have a halfpenny-worth of
pepper.   295

WIFE
That's a good boy. See, the little boy can hit it; by my troth,
it's a fine child.

RAFE
Relieve her with all courteous language. Now shut up shop;
no more my prentice, but my trusty squire and dwarf. I
must bespeak my shield and arming pestle.   300

                              [*Exeunt* TIM *and* GEORGE]

CITIZEN
Go thy ways, Rafe. As I'm a true man, thou art the best on
'em all.
WIFE
Rafe, Rafe.
RAFE
What say you, mistress?
WIFE
I prithee come again quickly, sweet Rafe.   305
RAFE
By and by.   *Exit* RAFE

        Enter JASPER *and his mother,* MISTRESS MERRYTHOUGHT

MISTRESS MERRYTHOUGHT
Give thee my blessing? No, I'll ne'er give thee my blessing;
I'll see thee hanged first; it shall ne'er be said I gave thee my
blessing. Th'art thy father's own son, of the right blood of
the Merrythoughts. I may curse the time that e'er I knew   310
thy father; he hath spent all his own, and mine too, and
when I tell him of it, he laughs and dances, and sings, and
cries, 'A merry heart lives long-a'. And thou art a wastethrift, and art run away from thy master that loved thee
well, and art come to me; and I have laid up a little for my   315
younger son Michael, and thou think'st to bezzle that, but
thou shalt never be able to do it.

---

300 *arming* armorial
313 'A merry heart lives long-a' a line from the song sung by Autolycus in *The
     Winter's Tale*, IV.iii, and by Silence in *2 Henry IV*, V.iii
313–14 *wastethrift* spendthrift
316 *bezzle* squander

Enter MICHAEL

– Come hither, Michael; come, Michael, down on thy
knees; thou shalt have my blessing.

MICHAEL

I pray you, mother, pray to God to bless me.   320

MISTRESS MERRYTHOUGHT

God bless thee; but Jasper shall never have my blessing. He
shall be hanged first, shall he not, Michael? How say'st
thou!

MICHAEL

Yes, forsooth, mother, and grace of God.

MISTRESS MERRYTHOUGHT

That's a good boy.   325

WIFE

I'faith, it's a fine spoken child.

JASPER

Mother, though you forget a parent's love,
I must preserve the duty of a child.
I ran not from my master, nor return
To have your stock maintain my idleness.   330

WIFE

Ungracious child, I warrant him; hark how he chops logic
with his mother! – Thou hadst best tell her she lies; do, tell
her she lies.

CITIZEN

If he were my son, I would hang him up by the heels, and
flay him, and salt him, whoreson halter-sack!   335

JASPER

My coming only is to beg your love,
Which I must ever, though I never gain it.
And howsoever you esteem of me,
There is no drop of blood hid in these veins
But I remember well belongs to you   340
That brought me forth, and would be glad for you
To rip them all again, and let it out.

MISTRESS MERRYTHOUGHT

I'faith, I had sorrow enough for thee, God knows; but I'll

331 *chops logic* bandies arguments
335 *halter-sack* gallows-bird
343 *sorrow* pain in child-birth

hamper thee well enough. Get thee in, thou vagabond, get
thee in, and learn of thy brother Michael.   345

[*Exeunt* JASPER *and* MICHAEL]

OLD MERRYTHOUGHT ([*sings*] *within*)
    Nose, nose, jolly red nose,
    And who gave thee this jolly red nose?
MISTRESS MERRYTHOUGHT
Hark, my husband; he's singing and hoiting, and I'm fain
to cark and care, and all little enough. – Husband, Charles,
Charles Merrythought.   350

Enter OLD MERRYTHOUGHT

OLD MERRYTHOUGHT [*sings*]
    Nutmegs and ginger, cinnamon and cloves,
    And they gave me this jolly red nose.
MISTRESS MERRYTHOUGHT
If you would consider your state, you would have little list
to sing, iwis.
OLD MERRYTHOUGHT
It should never be considered while it were an estate, if I   355
thought it would spoil my singing.
MISTRESS MERRYTHOUGHT
But how wilt thou do, Charles? Thou art an old man, and
thou canst not work, and thou hast not forty shillings left,
and thou eatest good meat, and drinkest good drink, and
laughest?   360
OLD MERRYTHOUGHT
And will do.
MISTRESS MERRYTHOUGHT
But how wilt thou come by it, Charles?
OLD MERRYTHOUGHT
How? Why, how have I done hitherto this forty years? I
never came into my dining room, but at eleven and six
o'clock I found excellent meat and drink o'th'table; my   365
clothes were never worn out, but next morning a tailor

344 *hamper* beat
346–52 *Nose ... nose* the refrain to a song from Thomas Ravenscroft's *Deuteromelia*
    (1609), no. 7; reprinted in Chappell, I. 141–2
348 *hoiting* roistering
349 *cark* fret
353 *state* estate, dignity
    list desire
354 *iwis* for certain
364–5 *eleven and six o'clock* the hours of the two main meals

brought me a new suit; and without question it will be so
ever. Use makes perfectness. If all should fail, it is but a
little straining myself extraordinary, and laugh myself to
death.   370

WIFE
    It's a foolish old man this: is not he, George?
CITIZEN
    Yes, cony.
WIFE
    Give me a penny i'th'purse while I live, George.
CITIZEN
    Ay, by lady, cony, hold thee there.

MISTRESS MERRYTHOUGHT
    Well, Charles, you promised to provide for Jasper, and I   375
    have laid up for Michael. I pray you, pay Jasper his portion;
    he's come home, and he shall not consume Michael's stock.
    He says his master turned him away, but I promise you
    truly, I think he ran away.

WIFE
    No, indeed, Mistress Merrythought, though he be a notable   380
    gallows, yet I'll assure you his master did turn him away,
    even in this place; 'twas, i'faith, within this half hour, about
    his daughter; my husband was by.
CITIZEN
    Hang him, rogue. He served him well enough: love his
    master's daughter! By my troth, cony, if there were a   385
    thousand boys, thou wouldst spoil them all with taking
    their parts. Let his mother alone with him.
WIFE
    Ay, George, but yet truth is truth.

368   *Use makes perfectness* (Tilley U24)
373   *Give ... live* Let me always be prudent
374   *hold thee there* stick to that
376   *laid up* saved money
        portion share of property given to an heir
380–1   *notable gallows* notorious gallows-bird
387   *parts* pun on roles and sexual organs
388   *truth is truth* proverbial (Tilley T581)

OLD MERRYTHOUGHT

Where is Jasper? He's welcome how ever. Call him in; he
shall have his portion. Is he merry?   390

MISTRESS MERRYTHOUGHT

Ay, foul chive him, he is too merry. – Jasper! Michael!

Enter JASPER *and* MICHAEL

OLD MERRYTHOUGHT

Welcome, Jasper, though thou run'st away, welcome; God
bless thee. 'Tis thy mother's mind thou shouldst receive thy
portion; thou hast been abroad, and I hope hast learned
experience enough to govern it; thou art of sufficient years. 395
Hold thy hand: one, two, three, four, five, six, seven, eight,
nine, there's ten shillings for thee. Thrust thyself into the
world with that, and take some settled course. If fortune
cross thee, thou hast a retiring place; come home to me; I
have twenty shillings left. Be a good husband, that is, wear 400
ordinary clothes, eat the best meat, and drink the best
drink; be merry, and give to the poor, and believe me, thou
hast no end of thy goods.

JASPER

Long may you live free from all thought of ill,
And long have cause to be thus merry still.   405
But, father –

OLD MERRYTHOUGHT

No more words, Jasper, get thee gone; thou hast my
blessing; thy father's spirit upon thee. Farewell, Jasper.
[*sings*]
> But yet, or ere you part, oh cruel,
> Kiss me, kiss me, sweeting, mine own dear jewel.   410
So, now begone; no words.

Exit JASPER

389 *how ever* in any case
391 *foul chive* ill betide
391 s.d. *Enter* ... MICHAEL (Q1 prints below line 388)
394–405 *thou ... still* 'a parody of the opening scene in Dekker's *Old Fortunatus*
(1599)' (Gurr)
399 *cross* thwart
400 *Be ... husband* Be thrifty and prudent
409–10 *But ... jewel* from a song 'Wilt thou, unkind, thus reave me of my heart' (no.
xv) in John Dowland's *The First Booke of Songes or Ayres* (1597), transcribed
in E. M. Fellowes, *The English School of Lutenist Song Writers* (London, 1921),
First Series, ii. 60–1; see Poulton, p. 235

MISTRESS MERRYTHOUGHT
  So, Michael, now get thee gone too.
MICHAEL
  Yes forsooth, mother; but I'll have my father's blessing first.
MISTRESS MERRYTHOUGHT
  No, Michael, 'tis no matter for his blessing; thou hast my
  blessing; begone. I'll fetch my money and jewels and follow   415
  thee; I'll stay no longer with him, I warrant thee.

                                        Exit MICHAEL

  – Truly, Charles, I'll be gone too.   *Not a happy*
OLD MERRYTHOUGHT   *marriage*
  What! You will not?
MISTRESS MERRYTHOUGHT
  Yes, indeed will I.
OLD MERRYTHOUGHT [*sings*]
        Hey-ho, farewell, Nan,   420
        I'll never trust wench more again, if I can.
MISTRESS MERRYTHOUGHT
  You shall not think, when all your own is gone, to spend
  that I have been scraping up for Michael.
OLD MERRYTHOUGHT
  Farewell, good wife, I expect it not; all I have to do in this
  world is to be merry; which I shall, if the ground be not   425
  taken from me; and if it be, [*sings*]
        When earth and seas from me are reft,
        The skies aloft for me are left.

                                        Exeunt

                    Finis Actus primi

414 *no matter* Q2 (now matter Q1)

427–8 a snatch from the ballad 'In Crete when Daedalus First Began'; text in H. E.
    Rollins, 'A "Recovered" Elizabethan Ballad', *RES*, 3 (1927), 336–7; music in
    Simpson, pp. 362–5.

427 *reft* p.p. of 'reave', take away

[Interlude I]

BOY *danceth. Music.*

WIFE

I'll be sworn he's a merry old gentleman for all that. Hark,
hark, husband, hark! Fiddles, fiddles! Now surely they go
finely. They say 'tis present death for these fiddlers to tune
their rebecks before the great Turk's grace, is't not, George!
But look, look, here's a youth dances. – Now, good youth,   5
do a turn o'th' toe. – Sweetheart, i'faith, I'll have Rafe come
and do some of his gambols. – He'll ride the wild mare,
gentlemen, 'twould do your hearts good to see him. – I
thank you, kind youth; pray, bid Rafe come.

CITIZEN

Peace, cony – Sirrah, you scurvy boy, bid the players send   10
Rafe, or by God's — and they do not, I'll tear some of their
periwigs beside their heads: this is all riff-raff.

[*Exit* BOY]

0 s.d. Dancing and music were customary in the interludes between the acts of a
  play, particularly in the private playhouses (see Chambers, II. 556–7).
2 *fiddles* these could be any stringed instrument of the time; violins were beginning
  to appear as well as viols
3–4 *They ... grace* Sultans were proverbially fearsome despots; Fynes Moryson,
  who had been in Turkey in 1595, wrote of the Emperor Amurath (1574–95):
  'He loved music, but had not the patience to attend the tuning of instruments',
  Itinerary, ed. C. Hughes (London, 1903), I. i, 4.
3 *present* immediate
4 *rebecks* early form of fiddle with three strings
7 *wild mare* see-saw, with suggestive connotations
11 The word omitted is probably 'body' – the 'Act to Restrain the Abuses of the
  Players' (3 James, Ch. 21) of 1606 had sought to quell profanity; but cf. II, 230
  where Humphrey swears by the sacrament, the sign of a swell.
12 *periwigs* frequently worn by actors at this time (Hattaway, pp. 81, 84–5)
  riff-raff rubbish

Act II

Enter MERCHANT *and* HUMPHREY

MERCHANT
  And how, faith, how goes it now, son Humphrey!
HUMPHREY
  Right worshipful, and my beloved friend
  And father dear, this matter's at an end.
MERCHANT
  'Tis well; it should be so; I'm glad the girl
  Is found so tractable.
HUMPHREY   Nay, she must whirl   5
  From hence (and you must wink; for so, I say,
  The story tells) tomorrow before day.

WIFE
  George, dost thou think in thy conscience now 'twill be a
  match? Tell me but what thou think'st, sweet rogue. Thou
  seest the poor gentleman, dear heart, how it labours and   10
  throbs, I warrant you, to be at rest. I'll go move the father
  for't.
CITIZEN
  No, no, I prithee sit still, honeysuckle; thou'lt spoil all. If he
  deny him, I'll bring half a dozen good fellows myself, and
  in the shutting of an evening knock't up, and there's an end.   15
WIFE
  I'll buss thee for that, i'faith, boy. Well, George, well, you
  have been a wag in your days, I warrant you; but God
  forgive you, and I do with all my heart.

MERCHANT
  How was it, son? You told me that tomorrow
  Before day break you must convey her hence?   20
HUMPHREY
  I must, I must, and thus it is agreed:
  Your daughter rides upon a brown-bay steed,
  I on a sorrel, which I bought of Brian,

Act II ed. (Actus secundi Scoena prima Q1)
  6 *wink* turn a blind eye
  15 *shutting of an evening* close of day, i.e. a short time
      knock't up put an end to the business
  16 *buss* kiss
  23 *sorrel* chestnut horse

The honest host of the Red Roaring Lion,
In Waltham situate. Then, if you may,   25
Consent in seemly sort, lest by delay
The fatal sisters come and do the office,
And then you'll sing another song.
MERCHANT   Alas,
Why should you be thus full of grief to me,
That do as willing as yourself agree   30
To anything, so it be good and fair?
Then steal her when you will, if such a pleasure
Content you both; I'll sleep and never see it,
To make your joys more full. But tell me why
You may not here perform your marriage?   35

WIFE

God's blessing o'thy soul, old man! I'faith, thou art loath to
part true hearts, I see. – 'A has her, George, and I'm as glad
on't. – Well, go thy ways, Humphrey, for a fair-spoken
man; I believe thou hast not thy fellow within the walls of
London; and I should say the suburbs too I should not lie.   40
– Why dost not rejoice with me, George?

CITIZEN

If I could but see Rafe again, I were as merry as mine host,
i'faith.

HUMPHREY

The cause you seem to ask, I thus declare
(Help me, oh Muses nine): your daughter sware   45
A foolish oath, the more it was the pity;
Yet none but myself within this city
Shall dare to say so, but a bold defiance
Shall meet him, were he of the noble science.
And yet she sware, and yet why did she swear?   50
Truly, I cannot tell, unless it were
For her own ease, for sure sometimes an oath,
Being sworn, thereafter is like cordial broth.
And this it was she swore: never to marry
But such a one whose mighty arm could carry   55
(As meaning me, for I am such a one)

27 *fatal sisters* the Fates, Clotho, Lachesis, and Atropos, of classical myth

29 *grief* grievance

40 *suburbs* For a description of these unsavoury areas just outside the walls where
   the citizens resorted for pleasure see Stow, ii. 69–97.

49 *science* of defence, i.e. boxing or fencing

53 *cordial* restorative

Her bodily away through stick and stone,
Till both of us arrive, at her request,
Some ten miles off, in the wild Waltham Forest.
MERCHANT
If this be all, you shall not need to fear   60
Any denial in your love. Proceed;
I'll neither follow nor repent the deed.
HUMPHREY
Good night, twenty good nights, and twenty more.
And twenty more good nights – that makes threescore.

Exeunt

Enter MISTRESS MERRYTHOUGHT [*with jewel casket
and purse of money*], *and her son* MICHAEL

MISTRESS MERRYTHOUGHT
Come, Michael; art thou not weary, boy?   65
MICHAEL
No, forsooth, mother, not I.
MISTRESS MERRYTHOUGHT
Where be we now, child?
MICHAEL
Indeed, forsooth, mother, I cannot tell, unless we be at Mile
End. Is not all the world Mile End, mother?
MISTRESS MERRYTHOUGHT
No, Michael, not all the world, boy; but I can assure thee,   70
Michael, Mile End is a goodly matter; there has been a
pitch-field, my child, between the naughty Spaniels and the
Englishmen; and the Spaniels ran away, Michael, and the

63–4 For possible parodies in these lines see Baldwin Maxwell, ' "Twenty Good
Nights" – *The Knight of the Burning Pestle* and Middleton's *Family of Love*',
MLN, LXIII (1948), 233–7; and W. J. Olive, ' "Twenty Good Nights" – *The
Knight of the Burning Pestle, The Family of Love*, and *Romeo and Juliet*', *SP*,
XLVII (1950), 182–9.

68–9 *Mile End* A hamlet one mile from Aldgate used as a training-ground for the
citizen forces. Entertainments were also held there, including mock-battles like
the one described in the Fiddler's ballad in *Monsieur Thomas*, III.iii: 'The
Landing of the Spaniards at Bow, with the Bloody Battle at Mile-End'. This is
probably the incident to which Mistress Merrythought refers.

72 *pitch-field* regular battle
naughty wicked
Spaniels she means Spaniards, although perhaps it is bawdy (a 'spaniel' could
designate a whore)

Englishmen followed. My neighbour Coxstone was there,
boy, and killed them all with a birding-piece.   75

MICHAEL

Mother, forsooth –

MISTRESS MERRYTHOUGHT

What says my white boy?

MICHAEL

Shall not my father go with us too?

MISTRESS MERRYTHOUGHT

No, Michael, let thy father go snick up; he shall never come
between a pair of sheets with me again while he lives. Let   80
him stay at home and sing for his supper, boy. Come, child,
sit down, and I'll show my boy fine knacks indeed. Look
here, Michael, here's a ring, and here's a brooch, and here's
a bracelet, and here's two rings more, and here's money and
gold by th'eye, my boy.   85

MICHAEL

Shall I have all this, mother?

MISTRESS MERRYTHOUGHT

Ay, Michael, thou shalt have all, Michael.

CITIZEN

How lik'st thou this, wench?

WIFE

I cannot tell; I would have Rafe, George; I'll see no more
else, indeed la, and I pray you let the youths understand so   90
much by word of mouth; for I tell you truly, I'm afraid o'
my boy. Come, come, George, let's be merry and wise. The
child's a fatherless child; and say they should put him into
a strait pair of gaskins, 'twere worse than knot-grass: he
would never grow after it.   95

74–5 Coxstone ... birding-piece bawdy; (a birding-piece was a light gun for shoot-
    ing game)

77 white darling

79 snick up hang himself

82 knacks trinkets

85 by th'eye in unlimited quantities

90 la (used for emphasis)
   youths boy actors

91 o' for

92 merry and wise Compare the proverb 'Good to be merry and wise' (Tilley G324)
   – with the implication that it is hard to be both.

94 strait tight
   gaskins breeches
   knot-grass supposed to stunt growth; cf. A Midsummer Night's Dream, III.ii.329

Enter RAFE, [TIM *as*] *Squire, and* [GEORGE *as*] *Dwarf*

CITIZEN

Here's Rafe, here's Rafe.

WIFE

How do you, Rafe? You are welcome, Rafe, as I may say;
it's a good boy, hold up thy head, and be not afraid; we are
thy friends, Rafe; the gentlemen will praise thee, Rafe, if
thou play'st thy part with audacity. Begin, Rafe, o'God's   100
name.

RAFE

My trusty squire, unlace my helm; give me my hat. Where
are we, or what desert may this be?

GEORGE

Mirror of knighthood, this is, as I take it, the perilous
Waltham Down, in whose bottom stands the enchanted   105
valley.

MISTRESS MERRYTHOUGHT

Oh Michael, we are betrayed, we are betrayed! Here be
giants! Fly, boy; fly, boy; fly!

Exeunt Mother and MICHAEL [*dropping purse and casket*]

RAFE

Lace on my helm again. What noise is this?
A gentle lady flying the embrace   110
Of some uncourteous knight? I will relieve her.
Go, squire, and say, the knight that wears this pestle
In honour of all ladies, swears revenge
Upon that recreant coward that pursues her.
Go comfort her, and that same gentle squire   115
That bears her company.

TIM   I go, brave knight.   [*Exit*]

RAFE

My trusty dwarf and friend, reach me my shield,
And hold it while I swear. First by my knighthood;
Then by the soul of Amadis de Gaul,
My famous ancestor; then by my sword   120

---

104 Henceforward Q1 substitutes the speech prefix DWARF for GEORGE
    Mirror of knighthood see I, 229n.

114 *recreant* cowardly, false

116 Henceforward Q1 substitutes the speech prefix SQUIRE for TIM

119 *Amadis de Gaul* Hero of the Iberian romance of that name (1508); the English
    translation by Antony Munday appeared in parts from 1590–1618

The beauteous Brionella girt about me;
By this bright burning pestle, of mine honour
The living trophy; and by all respect
Due to distressèd damsels: here I vow
Never to end the quest of this fair lady   125
And that forsaken squire, till by my valour
I gain their liberty.
GEORGE   Heaven bless the knight
That thus relieves poor errant gentlewomen.

Exeunt

WIFE
Ay, marry, Rafe, this has some savour in't. – I would see the
proudest of them all offer to carry his books after him. But,   130
George, I will not have him go away so soon; I shall be sick
if he go away, that I shall. Call Rafe again, George, call
Rafe again; I prithee, sweetheart, let him come fight before
me, and let's ha' some drums and some trumpets, and let
him kill all that comes near him, and thou lov'st me,   135
George.
CITIZEN
Peace a little, bird; he shall kill them all, and they were
twenty more on 'em than there are.

Enter JASPER

JASPER
Now, Fortune, if thou be'st not only ill,
Show me thy better face, and bring about   140
Thy desperate wheel, that I may climb at length
And stand. This is our place of meeting,
If love have any constancy. Oh age,
Where only wealthy men are counted happy!
How shall I please thee, how deserve thy smiles,   145
When I am only rich in misery?
My father's blessing, and this little coin
Is my inheritance, a strong revènue!

---

121 *Brionella* The mistress of Palmerin's (see I, 211n.) friend Ptolome (Murch)
128 s.d. *Exeunt* ed. (*Exit* Q1)
130 *carry his books* follow like a lowly pedant; cf. Tilley B533
139 *ill* both ugly and unlucky
140–41 *better .... wheel* The goddess Fortuna, sometimes depicted Janus-faced, was
   customarily shown turning a wheel, signifying the short life of man's felicity (see
   Frederick Kiefer, *Fortune and Elizabethan Tragedy* (San Marino, Ca., 1983)).

From earth thou art, and to the earth I give thee.

                        [*Casts the money away*] Wtf

There grow and multiply, whilst fresher air   150
Breeds me a fresher fortune. – How, illusion!

                      Spies the casket

What, hath the devil coined himself before me?
'Tis metal good, it rings well; I am waking,
And taking too, I hope. Now God's dear blessing
Upon his heart that left it here. 'Tis mine;   155
These pearls, I take it, were not left for swine.   *Exit*

WIFE

I do not like that this unthrifty youth should embezzle away
the money; the poor gentlewoman his mother will have a
heavy heart for it, God knows.

CITIZEN

And reason good, sweetheart.   160

WIFE

But let him go. I'll tell Rafe a tale in's ear shall fetch him
again with a wanion, I warrant him, if he be above ground;
and besides, George, here are a number of sufficient
gentlemen can witness, and myself, and yourself, and the
musicians, if we be called in question. But here comes Rafe,   165
George; thou shalt hear him speak, an he were an emperal.

        Enter RAFE *and* [GEORGE *as*] *Dwarf*

RAFE

Comes not Sir Squire again?

149 A parody of the parable of the talents where one of the servants buried his lord's
    money in the ground, Matthew xxv.14 ff.
    to the earth Q1 (to earth Q3, F)
152 *coined* formed
153–4 *waking ... taking* becoming aware and comprehending
157 *embezzle* squander
162 *wanion* vengeance
163 *sufficient* able
166 *an* as if
    emperal solecism for emperor
167 With this episode compare *Palmerin d'Oliva*, I.xxi: 'How Palmerin and Ptolome
    met with a damsel who made great moan for a casket which two knights had
    forcibly taken from her, and what happened to them', trans. A. Munday
    (London, 1588).

GEORGE   Right courteous knight,
  Your squire doth come and with him comes the lady,

      Enter MISTRESS MERRYTHOUGHT *and* MICHAEL,
            and [TIM *as*] *Squire*

For and the Squire of Damsels, as I take it.
RAFE
  Madam, if any service or devoir   170
  Of a poor errant knight may right your wrongs,
  Command it; I am prest to give you succour,
  For to that holy end I bear my armour.
MISTRESS MERRYTHOUGHT
  Alas, sir, I am a poor gentlewoman, and I have lost my
  money in this forest.   175
RAFE
  Desert, you would say, lady, and not lost
  Whilst I have sword and lance. Dry up your tears,
  Which ill befits the beauty of that face,
  And tell the story, if I may request it,
  Of your disastrous fortune.   180
MISTRESS MERRYTHOUGHT
  Out, alas! I left a thousand pound, a thousand pound, e'en
  all the money I had laid up for this youth, upon the sight of
  your mastership; you looked so grim, and, as I may say it,
  saving your presence, more like a giant than a mortal man.
RAFE
  I am as you are, lady; so are they   185
  All mortal. But why weeps this gentle squire?
MISTRESS MERRYTHOUGHT
  Has he not cause to weep, do you think, when he hath
  lost his inheritance?
RAFE
  Young hope of valour, weep not; I am here
  That will confound thy foe and pay it dear   190
  Upon his coward head, that dares deny
  Distressèd squires and ladies equity.

---

169 *For and* As well as
    the Squire of Damsels In Spenser's *The Faerie Queene*, III.vii.51 ff. the Squire of
    Dames has to find three hundred ladies who will 'abide for euer chaste and
    sound'. When Satyrane meets him he has found three.
170 *devoir* duty
172 *prest* prepared (French *prêt*)
178 *befits* For the singular inflection, see Abbott 333–9.
186 *All* Wholly
192 *equity* justice

I have but one horse, on which shall ride
This lady fair behind me, and before
This courteous squire; fortune will give us more   195
Upon our next adventure. Fairly speed
Beside us, squire and dwarf, to do us need.

                                        Exeunt

CITIZEN

Did not I tell you, Nell, what your man would do? By the
faith of my body, wench, for clean action and good delivery
they may all cast their caps at him.   200

WIFE

And so they may, i'faith, for I dare speak it boldly, the
twelve companies of London cannot match him, timber for
timber. Well, George, and he be not inveigled by some of
these paltry players, I ha' much marvel; but, George, we ha'
done our parts if the boy have any grace to be thankful.   205

CITIZEN

Yes, I warrant thee, duckling.

                    Enter HUMPHREY *and* LUCE

HUMPHREY

Good Mistress Luce, however I in fault am
For your lame horse, you're welcome unto Waltham.
But which way now to go or what to say
I know not truly till it be broad day.   210

LUCE

Oh fear not, Master Humphrey, I am guide
For this place good enough.

HUMPHREY   Then up and ride,
Or, if it please you, walk for your repose,
Or sit, or if you will, go pluck a rose;

199 *clean* nifty

200 *cast their caps at him* despair of imitating (Tilley C62)

202 *the twelve companies* These were the Mercers, the Grocers, the Drapers, the
   Fishmongers, the Goldsmiths, the Skinners, the Merchant Tailors, the
   Haberdashers, the Salters, the Ironmongers, the Vintners, and the Clothworkers;
   see Steven Rappaport, *Worlds within Worlds: Structures of Life in Sixteenth
   Century London* (Cambridge, 1989).

202–3 *timber for timber* like for like

203 *inveigled* Masters of the boy troupes on occasion kidnapped likely actors (see
   Harbage, p. 40).

214 *go pluck a rose* make water (Tilley R184)

Either of which shall be indifferent   215
To your good friend and Humphrey, whose consent
Is so entangled ever to your will,
As the poor harmless horse is to the mill.
LUCE
Faith, and you say the word, we'll e'en sit down
And take a nap.
HUMPHREY   'Tis better in the town,   220
Where we may nap together; for, believe me,
To sleep without a snatch would mickle grieve me.
LUCE   fuck
You're merry, Master Humphrey.
HUMPHREY   So I am,
And have been ever merry from my dam.
LUCE
Your nurse had the less labour.
HUMPHREY   Faith, it may be,   225
Unless it were by chance I did beray me.

                        Enter JASPER

JASPER
Luce, dear friend Luce!
LUCE   Here, Jasper.
JASPER   You are mine.
HUMPHREY
If it be so, my friend, you use me fine;
What do you think I am?
JASPER   An arrant noddy.
HUMPHREY
A word of obloquy! Now, by God's body,   230
I'll tell thy master, for I know thee well.
JASPER
Nay, and you be so forward for to tell,
Take that, and that, and tell him, sir, I gave it, [*Beats him*]
And say I paid you well.
HUMPHREY   Oh, sir, I have it,
And do confess the payment. Pray be quiet.   235
JASPER
Go, get to your night-cap and the diet

221 *nap* pun meaning both sleep and drink
222 *snatch* snack, also a hasty coupling
226 *beray me* befoul myself
230 *by God's body* See Interlude I, 11n.
235 *confess* acknowledge
     quiet at peace

To cure your beaten bones.
LUCE   Alas, poor Humphrey,
  Get thee some wholesome broth with sage and comfrey;
  A little oil of roses and a feather
  To 'noint thy back withal.
HUMPHREY   When I came hither   240
  Would I had gone to Paris with John Dory.
LUCE
  Farewell, my pretty Nump; I am very sorry
  I cannot bear thee company.
HUMPHREY   Farewell;
  The devil's dam was ne'er so banged in hell.

                    Exeunt [LUCE *and* JASPER]
                    Manet HUMPHREY

WIFE
  This young Jasper will prove me another thing, o'my   245
  conscience, and he may be suffered. George, dost not see,
  George, how 'a swaggers, and flies at the very heads o'folks
  as he were a dragon? Well, if I do not do his lesson for
  wronging the poor gentleman, I am no true woman. His
  friends that brought him up might have been better   250
  occupied, iwis, than ha' taught him these fegaries; he's e'en
  in the highway to the gallows, God bless him.
CITIZEN
  You're too bitter, cony; the young man may do well enough
  for all this.
WIFE
  Come hither, Master Humphrey; has he hurt you? Now   255
  beshrew his fingers for't. Here, sweetheart, here's some
  green ginger for thee. Now beshrew my heart, but 'a has a

---

238 *comfrey* plant common near ditches and streams and supposed to have healing
     virtues
241 *John Dory* In a ballad of this title (music by Ravenscroft [*Deuteromelia*, 1609]
     reprinted in Simpson, pp. 398–400) the hero is captured while on his way to the
     King of France with a crew of English 'churls'.
242 *Nump* fool and pet-name for Humphrey
244 *devil's dam* Humphrey is probably thinking of a morality play in which the devil
     and his crew were belaboured by the vices.
244 s.d. 2 *Manet* Remains on stage
245 *thing* ed. (things Q1)
246 *and … suffered* if he is allowed to continue in this manner
251 *fegaries* vagaries, pranks
257 *has a* ed. (has Q1)

peppernel in's head as big as a pullet's egg. Alas, sweet
lamb, how thy temples beat! Take the peace on him, sweetheart, take the peace on him.   260

CITIZEN

No, no, you talk like a foolish woman. I'll ha' Rafe fight
with him, and swinge him up well-favouredly. – Sirrah boy,
come hither!

Enter a BOY

Let Rafe come in and fight with Jasper.

WIFE

Ay, and beat him well; he's an unhappy boy.   265

BOY

Sir, you must pardon us; the plot of our play lies contrary,
and 'twill hazard the spoiling of our play.

CITIZEN

Plot me no plots. I'll ha' Rafe come out; I'll make your
house too hot for you else.

BOY

Why, sir, he shall; but if anything fall out of order, the   270
gentlemen must pardon us.

CITIZEN

Go your ways, goodman boy.

                                                    [*Exit* BOY]

– I'll hold him a penny he shall have his belly-ful of fighting
now. Ho, here comes Rafe; no more.

Enter RAFE, MISTRESS MERRYTHOUGHT, MICHAEL, [TIM
as] *Squire, and* [GEORGE *as*] *Dwarf*

RAFE

What knight is that, squire? Ask him if he keep   275
The passage, bound by love of lady fair,
Or else but prickant.

HUMPHREY   Sir, I am no knight,
But a poor gentleman, that this same night

---

258 *peppernel* lump
259 *Take the peace* Obtain sureties for his good conduct
262 *swinge* thrash
   well-favouredly handsomely, thoroughly
263 s.d. after 260 Q1
265 *unhappy* 'mischievously waggish' (Johnson); cf. *All's Well*, IV.v.67
273 *hold* bet
275–6 *keep ... passage* guard the entrance to a castle

Had stolen from me on yonder green
My lovely wife, and suffered (to be seen   280
Yet extant on my shoulders) such a greeting
That whilst I live I shall think of that meeting.

WIFE
   Ay, Rafe, he beat him unmercifully, Rafe; and thou spar'st
   him, Rafe, I would thou wert hanged.
CITIZEN
   No more, wife, no more.   285

RAFE
   Where is the caitiff wretch hath done this deed?
   Lady, your pardon, that I may proceed
   Upon the quest of this injurious knight.
   And thou, fair squire, repute me not the worse,
   In leaving the great venture of the purse   290
   And the rich casket till some better leisure.

Enter JASPER *and* LUCE

HUMPHREY
   Here comes the broker hath purloined my treasure.
RAFE
   Go, squire, and tell him I am here,
   An errant knight at arms, to crave delivery
   Of that fair lady to her own knight's arms.   295
   If he deny, bid him take choice of ground,
   And so defy him.
TIM   From the knight that bears
   The golden pestle, I defy thee, knight,
   Unless thou make fair restitution
   Of that bright lady.
JASPER   Tell the knight that sent thee   290
   He is an ass, and I will keep the wench
   And knock his head-piece.
RAFE   Knight, thou art but dead,
   If thou recall not thy uncourteous terms.

WIFE
   Break's pate, Rafe; break's pate, Rafe, soundly.

---

286 *caitiff* wicked
288 *injurious* malicious
292 *broker* pimp
303 *thou* Q2 (thou thou Q1)

JASPER
   Come, knight, I am ready for you. Now your pestle   305

                    Snatches away his pestle

Shall try what temper, sir, your mortar's of.
[*Recites*] 'With that he stood upright in his stirrups, and
gave the Knight of the Calf-skin such a knock
                              [*Knocks* RAFE *down*]
that he forsook his horse and down he fell; and then he
leaped upon him, and plucking off his helmet –'   310
HUMPHREY
   Nay, and my noble knight be down so soon,
   Though I can scarcely go, I needs must run.

         Exeunt HUMPHREY *and* RAFE [*with* TIM *and* GEORGE]

WIFE
   Run, Rafe; run, Rafe; run for thy life, boy; Jasper comes,
   Jasper comes.

JASPER
   Come, Luce, we must have other arms for you;   315
   Humphrey and Golden Pestle, both adieu.

                    Exeunt [JASPER *and* LUCE]

WIFE
   Sure the devil, God bless us, is in this springald. Why,
   George, didst ever see such a fire-drake? I am afraid my
   boy's miscarried; if he be, though he were Master
   Merrythought's son a thousand times, if there be any law in   320
   England, I'll make some of them smart for't.
CITIZEN
   No, no, I have found out the matter, sweetheart: Jasper is
   enchanted; as sure as we are here, he is enchanted. He could

---

306 *mortar's* probably a reference to a helmet worn by Rafe
     of Q2 (off Q1)
307–10 printed as verse in Q1–3, F
308 *Calf-skin* The old romances were written on calf-skin or vellum.
312 *go* walk
312 s.d. *Exeunt* ed. (*Exit* Q1)
317 *springald* stripling
318 *fire-drake* 'A fire sometime seen, flying in the night, like a dragon', J. Bullokar,
     An English Expositor (London, 1616); cf. Brand, i. 235
319 *miscarried* come to harm

page of notes for exam

no more have stood in Rafe's hands than I can stand in my
Lord Mayor's. I'll have a ring to discover all enchantments,   325
and Rafe shall beat him yet. Be no more vexed, for it shall
be so.

Enter RAFE, [TIM *as*] *Squire,* [GEORGE *as*] *Dwarf,*
MISTRESS MERRYTHOUGHT *and* MICHAEL

WIFE
Oh, husband, here's Rafe again. – Stay, Rafe, let me speak
with thee. How dost thou, Rafe? Art thou not shroadly
hurt? The foul great lungies laid unmercifully on thee;   330
there's some sugar-candy for thee. Proceed, thou shalt have
another bout with him.

CITIZEN
If Rafe had him at the fencing-school, if he did not make a
puppy of him, and drive him up and down the school, he
should ne'er come in my shop more.   335

MISTRESS MERRYTHOUGHT
Truly, Master Knight of the Burning Pestle, I am weary.

MICHAEL
Indeed la, mother, and I am very hungry.

RAFE
Take comfort, gentle dame, and you, fair squire,
For in this desert there must needs be placed
Many strong castles held by courteous knights;   340
And till I bring you safe to one of those,
I swear by this my order ne'er to leave you.

WIFE
Well said, Rafe. – George, Rafe was ever comfortable, was
he not?

CITIZEN
Yes, duck.   345

WIFE
I shall ne'er forget him, when we had lost our child (you
know it was strayed almost, alone, to Puddle Wharf, and
the criers were abroad for it, and there it had drowned itself

---

329 *shroadly* obs. form of shrewdly, grievously
330 *lungies* <Longinus (who speared Christ), louts
334 *puppy* coward
342 *order* of knighthood
343 *comfortable* helpful
347 *Puddle Wharf* a landing place at the foot of St Andrew's Hill, now Puddle Dock

but for a sculler), Rafe was the most comfortablest to me:
'Peace, mistress', says he, 'let it go; I'll get you another as   350
good'. Did he not, George, did he not say so?   *So he's gonna have sex w/ her??*
CITIZEN
    Yes indeed did he, mouse.

GEORGE
    I would we had a mess of pottage and a pot of drink,
    squire, and were going to bed.
TIM
    Why, we are at Waltham town's end, and that's the Bell   355
    Inn.
GEORGE
    Take courage, valiant knight, damsel, and squire;
    I have discovered, not a stone's cast off,
    An ancient castle held by the old knight
    Of the most holy order of the Bell,   360
    Who gives to all knights errant entertain.
    There plenty is of food, and all prepared
    By the white hands of his own lady dear.
    He hath three squires that welcome all his guests:
    The first hight Chamberlino, who will see   365
    Our beds prepared, and bring us snowy sheets,
    Where never footman stretched his buttered hams;
    The second hight Tapstero, who will see
    Our pots full filled and no froth therein;
    The third, a gentle squire, Ostlero hight,   370
    Who will our palfreys slick with wisps of straw,
    And in the manger put them oats enough,
    And never grease their teeth with candle-snuff.

WIFE
    That same dwarf's a pretty boy, but the squire's a groutnoll.

---

349 *sculler* waterman
350 *get you* beget upon you
357 ff. With this episode compare Don Quixote's visit to the Inn on the first night of
      his wanderings (I.ii and iii).
365 *hight* ed. (high Q1) called
367 *never . . . hams* Footmen were servants who ran with their master's carriage; they
      greased their calves to prevent cramp.
368 *Tapstero* ed. (Tastero Q1, Tapstro Q2–3, F)
371 *slick* make sleek
373 *never . . . candle-snuff* a common trick to prevent the horses from eating; cf. *King
      Lear*, II.iv.124
374 *groutnoll* blockhead

RAFE

Knock at the gates, my squire, with stately lance.   375

[TIM *knocks*]

Enter TAPSTER

TAPSTER

Who's there? – You're welcome, gentlemen; will you see a room?

GEORGE

Right courteous and valiant Knight of the Burning Pestle, this is the Squire Tapstero.

RAFE

Fair Squire Tapstero, I, a wandering knight   380
Hight of the Burning Pestle, in the quest
Of this fair lady's casket and wrought purse,
Losing myself in this vast wilderness,
Am to this castle well by fortune brought;
Where, hearing of the goodly entertain   385
Your knight of holy order of the Bell
Gives to all damsels and all errant knights,
I thought to knock, and now am bold to enter.

TAPSTER

An't please you see a chamber, you are very welcome.

Exeunt

WIFE

George, I would have something done, and I cannot tell   390
what it is.

CITIZEN

What is it, Nell?

WIFE

Why, George, shall Rafe beat nobody again? Prithee, sweet-heart, let him.

CITIZEN

So he shall, Nell; and if I join with him, we'll knock them   395
all.

Enter HUMPHREY *and* MERCHANT

WIFE

Oh, George, here's Master Humphrey again now, that

382 *wrought* embroidered

lost Mistress Luce, and Mistress Luce's father. Master
Humphrey will do somebody's errand, I warrant him.

HUMPHREY
Father, it's true in arms I ne'er shall clasp her,   400
For she is stol'n away by your man Jasper.

WIFE
I thought he would tell him.

MERCHANT
Unhappy that I am to lose my child!
Now I begin to think on Jasper's words,
Who oft hath urged to me thy foolishness.   405
Why didst thou let her go? Thou lov'st her not,
That wouldst bring home thy life, and not bring her.
HUMPHREY
Father, forgive me. Shall I tell you true?
Look on my shoulders, they are black and blue.
Whilst to and fro fair Luce and I were winding,   410
He came and basted me with a hedge-binding.
MERCHANT
Get men and horses straight; we will be there
Within this hour. You know the place again?
HUMPHREY
I know the place where he my loins did swaddle.
I'll get six horses, and to each a saddle.   415
MERCHANT
Meantime I'll go talk with Jasper's father.

Exeunt

WIFE
George, what wilt thou lay with me now, that Master
Humphrey has not Mistress Luce yet? Speak, George, what
wilt thou lay with me?
CITIZEN
No, Nell, I warrant thee Jasper is at Puckeridge with her by   420
this.

---

399 *errand* ed. (errant Q1) *do ... errand* perform a worthy deed
411 *basted* beat
414 *swaddle* swathe, beat soundly
419 *lay* wager
420 *Puckeridge* a village in Hertfordshire, 23 miles N. of London

WIFE

Nay, George, you must consider Mistress Luce's feet are
tender, and, besides, 'tis dark; and I promise you truly, I do
not see how he should get out of Waltham Forest with her
yet.   425

CITIZEN

Nay, cony, what wilt thou lay with me that Rafe has her
not yet?

WIFE

I will not lay against Rafe, honey, because I have not
spoken with him. But look, George, peace; here comes the
merry old gentleman again.   430

Enter OLD MERRYTHOUGHT

OLD MERRYTHOUGHT [*sings*]

    When it was grown to dark midnight;
      And all were fast asleep,
    In came Margaret's grimly ghost,
      And stood at William's feet.

I have money and meat and drink beforehand till tomorrow   435
at noon; why should I be sad? Methinks I have half a dozen
jovial spirits within me. I am [*sings*]

    Three merry men, and three merry men.

To what end should any man be sad in this world? Give me
a man that when he goes to hanging cries [*sings*]:   440

    Troll the black bowl to me!

and a woman that will sing a catch in her travail. I have
seen a man come by my door with a serious face, in a black

431–4 *When . . . feet* a version of a stanza from 'Fair Margaret and Sweet William',
    Child No. 74, music in Simpson, pp. 785–8.

433 *grimly* grim-looking

437–8 *me. I am* / Three ed. (me. / I am three Q1)

438 *Three . . . men* from a song 'The Wise Men were but Seven' that appears in
    Twelfth Night, II.iii.77–8, Peele's *Old Wives' Tale,* 21–4, and is adapted in III.
    ii of Fletcher's *The Bloody Bother;* music in Chappell, I. 16

441 *Troll . . . me* A harvest song with this line appears in Nashe's *Summer's Last Will
    and Testament,* II.804 ff.; cf. the song for the end of *The Shoemaker's Holiday.*
    Music for a catch to '*Troll the bowl to me*' is found in Peter Warlock's tran-
    scription of *Pammelia and other Rounds and Catches by Thomas Ravenscroft*
    (Oxford, 1928), p. 14.
    Troll Pass

442 *catch* song in canon
    travail labour

cloak, without a hat-band, carrying his head as if he looked
for pins in the street; I have looked out of my window half   445
a year after, and have spied that man's head upon London
Bridge. 'Tis vile. Never trust a tailor that does not sing at
his work: his mind is of nothing but filching.

WIFE

Mark this, George, 'tis worth noting; Godfrey my tailor,
you know, never sings, and he had fourteen yards to make   450
this gown; and I'll be sworn Mistress Pennistone the
draper's wife had one made with twelve.

OLD MERRYTHOUGHT [*sings*]
    'Tis mirth that fills the veins with blood,
    More than wine, or sleep, or food;
    Let each man keep his heart at ease,   455
    No man dies of that disease.
    He that would his body keep
    From diseases, must not weep;
    But whoever laughs and sings,
    Never he his body brings   460
    Into fevers, gouts, or rheums,
    Or lingeringly his lungs consumes,
    Or meets with achès in the bone,
    Or catarrhs, or griping stone,
    But contented lives for aye;   465
    The more he laughs, the more he may.

WIFE

Look, George, how say'st thou by this, George? Is't not a
fine old man? – Now God's blessing o'thy sweet lips. –
When wilt thou be so merry, George? Faith, thou art the
frowning'st little thing, when thou art angry, in a country.   470

---

444 *hat-band* Hat-bands of rich materials were fashionable. Stubbes comments on 'a
    new fashion to wear them [hats?] without bands' (i. 51).
446–7 *head ... Bridge.* The heads of traitors were set on poles over the bridge gate
    until the reign of Charles II.
447 *tailor* tailors were proverbially dishonest
462 *lungs* Q3 (longs Q1)
463 *achès* pronounced 'aitches'
464 *griping* suddenly painful

Enter MERCHANT

CITIZEN

Peace, cony, thou shalt see him taken down too, I warrant
thee. Here's Luce's father come now.

OLD MERRYTHOUGHT [*sings*]
 As you came from Walsingham,
  From that holy land,
 There met you not with my true love   475
  By the way as you came?

MERCHANT

Oh, Master Merrythought, my daughter's gone!
This mirth becomes you not, my daughter's gone.

OLD MERRYTHOUGHT [*sings*]
 Why, an if she be, what care I?
 Or let her come, or go, or tarry.   480

MERCHANT

Mock not my misery; it is your son
Whom I have made my own, when all forsook him,
Has stol'n my only joy, my child, away.

OLD MERRYTHOUGHT [*sings*]
 He set her on a milk-white steed,
  And himself upon a grey,   485
 He never turned his face again,
  But he bore her quite away.

MERCHANT

Unworthy of the kindness I have shown
To thee and thine! Too late I well perceive
Thou art consenting to my daughter's loss.   490

473–6 *As ... came* a very popular ballad that exists in many versions; music in
 Simpson, pp. 741–3; Walsingham is a village in Norfolk, and until 1538 was a
 favourite place of pilgrimage to the shrine of the Virgin Mary
479–80 *Why ... tarry* From 'Farewell, Dear Love', a popular song that appears in
 Twelfth Night, II.iii.97 and is given in full with music in Robert Jones's *First
 Book of Songes and Ayres* (1600), reprinted in *The English Lute-Songs*, ed.
 Edmund H. Fellowes, revised by Thurston Dart, Series II, Vol. IV (London,
 1959), pp. 24–5; for 'farewell jigs', see Baskervill, pp. 180–7.
484–7 *He ... away* Corresponds to a stanza in 'The Ballad of the Knight and the
 Shepherd's Daughter', No. 110 in the Child Collection; music in Simpson, pp.
 658–9. As Child notes, however, Merrythought's stanza 'may equally well
 belong' to the ballad entitled 'The Douglas Tragedy', Child No. 7; music in
 Bronson, i. 106 ff.

what a strange man (handwritten margin note)

OLD MERRYTHOUGHT

Your daughter? What a stir's here wi'yer daughter? Let her
go, think no more on her, but sing loud. If both my sons
were on the gallows, I would sing, [*sings*]
> *Down, down, down they fall,*
> *Down; and arise they never shall.*   495

MERCHANT

Oh, might I behold her once again,
And she once more embrace her aged sire.

OLD MERRYTHOUGHT

Fie, how scurvily this goes. 'And she once more embrace
her aged sire?' You'll make a dog on her, will ye? She cares
much for her aged sire, I warrant you. [*sings*]   500
> *She cares not for her daddy, nor*
>   *She cares not for her mammy;*
> *For she is, she is, she is, she is*
>   *My Lord of Lowgave's lassie.*

MERCHANT

For this thy scorn, I will pursue that son   505
Of thine to death.

OLD MERRYTHOUGHT

Do, and when you ha' killed him, [*sings*]
> *Give him flowers enow, palmer, give him flowers*
>   *enow,*
> *Give him red, and white, and blue, green, and yellow.*

MERCHANT

I'll fetch my daughter.   510

OLD MERRYTHOUGHT

I'll hear no more o' your daughter; it spoils my mirth.

MERCHANT

I say, I'll fetch my daughter.

OLD MERRYTHOUGHT [*sings*]
> *Was never man for lady's sake,*
>   *Down, down,*
> *Tormented as I, poor Sir Guy?*   515

---

491   *wi'* F (wee Q1)
      yer Q1 (y'r F)

494–5   *Down ... shall* from 'Sorrow Stay,' No. III in John Dowland's *The Second
      Book of Songes and Ayres* (1600), reprinted with music in *The English School
      of Lutenist Song Writers*, ed. E. H. Fellowes (London, 1922), First Series, V,
      14–18; see Poulton, pp. 257–8

499   *make ... her* Venturewell has called himself Luce's 'sire'.

501   *cares* Q2 (cares cares Q1)

508   *palmer* pilgrim

513–20   *Was ... down* From the ballad of Guy of Warwick; see Simpson, pp. 283–5.

> *De derry down,*
> *For Lucy's sake, that lady bright,*
> *Down, down,*
> *As ever men beheld with eye?*
> *De derry down.*   520

MERCHANT
I'll be revenged, by heaven.

Exeunt

Finis Actus Secundi

[Interlude II]

Music

WIFE
How dost thou like this, George?
CITIZEN   roused
Why, this is well, cony; but if Rafe were hot once, thou
shouldst see more.
WIFE
The fiddlers go again, husband.
CITIZEN
Ay, Nell, but this is scurvy music. I gave the whoreson   5
gallows money, and I think he has not got me the waits of
Southwark. If I hear 'em not anon, I'll twinge him by the
ears. – You musicians, play 'Baloo'.
WIFE
No, good George, lets ha' 'Lachrimae'.
CITIZEN
Why, this is it, cony.   10
WIFE
It's all the better, George. Now, sweet lamb, what story is

2 *hot* roused
4 *go* are playing
7 *'em* ed. (him Q)
8 '*Baloo*' or 'balow', a word that occurs frequently in the refrains to lullabies; see
Simpson, pp. 31–4
9 '*Lachrimae*' an immensely popular set of pavanes by Dowland (1600); see
Poulton, pp. 125–32 where the music is transcribed
11–12 *story ... cloth* painted arras cloths, cheap imitations of tapestries, hung
behind the stage

that painted upon the cloth? 'The Confutation of Saint
Paul'?

CITIZEN

No, lamb, that's 'Rafe and Lucrece'.

WIFE

'Rafe and Lucrece'? Which Rafe? Our Rafe? 15

CITIZEN

No, mouse, that was a Tartarian.

WIFE

A Tartarian! Well, I would the fiddlers had done, that we
might see our Rafe again.

Act III

Enter JASPER *and* LUCE

JASPER

Come, my dear deer, though we have lost our way,
We have not lost ourselves. Are you not weary
With this night's wandering, broken from your rest,
And frighted with the terror that attends
The darkness of this wild unpeopled place? 5

LUCE

No, my best friend, I cannot either fear
Or entertain a weary thought, whilst you
(The end of all my full desires) stand by me.
Let them that lose their hopes, and live to languish
Amongst the number of forsaken lovers, 10
Tell the long weary steps, and number time,

12–13 *The ... Paul* a bawdy malapropism for 'The Conversion of Saint Paul'; cf.
Fr. *con* and Lat. *futuo*

14 *'Rafe ... Lucrece'* He means of course 'The Rape of Lucrece', the subject of
Shakespeare's poem (1594) and of a play by Heywood printed in 1608.

16 *Tartarian* another malapropism, for Sextus Tarquinius who raped Lucrece; the
Citizen might, however, be thinking of the proverbial cruelty of the inhabitants
of Tartary (north of the Caucasus and Himalayas) towards their women;
Tartarian is also a cant name for a thief

Act III ed. (Actus tertius, Scoena prima Q1)

1 *dear deer* ed. (deere deere Q1)
3 *broken* interrupted, roused
5 *this* Q2 (these Q1)
11 *Tell* Count

Start at a shadow, and shrink up their blood,
Whilst I (possessed with all content and quiet)
Thus take my pretty love, and thus embrace him.

JASPER
You have caught me, Luce, so fast, that whilst I live   15
I shall become your faithful prisoner
And wear these chains for ever. Come, sit down,
And rest your body, too, too delicate
For these disturbances. So, will you sleep?
Come, do not be more able than you are;   20
I know, you are not skilful in these watches,
For women are no soldiers; be not nice,
But take it; sleep, I say.

LUCE   I cannot sleep,
Indeed I cannot, friend.

JASPER   Why, then we'll sing,
And try how that will work upon our senses.   25

LUCE
I'll sing, or say, or anything but sleep.

JASPER
Come, little mermaid, rob me of my heart
With that enchanting voice.

LUCE   You mock me, Jasper.

Song

JASPER   *Tell me, dearest, what is love?*
LUCE   *'Tis a lightning from above,*   30
          'Tis an arrow, 'tis a fire,
          'Tis a boy they call Desire,
                'Tis a smile
                Doth beguile
JASPER   *The poor hearts of men that prove.*   35

12 *shrink ... blood* 'Fear diminished the cardiac "vital" spirits, according to medical teachings deriving from Avicenna' (Zitner)

17 *wear* Q2 (were Q1)

22 *nice* reluctant, fastidious

23 *take it* yield

26 *say* speak

27–8 *mermaid ... voice* Mermaids were associated with the Sirens who lured Ulysses with song.

28 *Song* Q1ᶜ (*Sung* Q1ᵘ)

29–42 *Tell ... anew* The original music for this song has survived and is reprinted by E. S. Lindsey, 'The Music of the Songs in Fletcher's Plays,' *SP*, XXI (1924), 331; the song also occurs in *The Captain*, II.ii.160 ff., with variations and an added stanza.

35 *prove* strive

	Tell me more, are women true?
LUCE	*Some love change, and so do you.*
JASPER	*Are they fair, and never kind?*
LUCE	*Yes, when men turn with the wind.*
JASPER	*Are they froward?*
LUCE	*Ever, toward*
	Those that love to love anew.

40

JASPER
  Dissemble it no more; I see the god
  Of heavy sleep lay on his heavy mace
  Upon your eyelids.

45

LUCE   I am very heavy.

[Sleeps]

JASPER
  Sleep, sleep, and quiet rest crown thy sweet thoughts.
  Keep from her fair blood distempers, startings,
  Horrors, and fearful shapes; let all her dreams
  Be joys, and chaste delights, embraces, wishes,
  And such new pleasures as the ravished soul
  Gives to the senses. So, my charms have took.
  Keep her, you powers divine, whilst I contemplate
  Upon the wealth and beauty of her mind.
  She is only fair and constant, only kind,
  And only to thee, Jasper. Oh my joys,
  Whither will you transport me? Let not fullness
  Of my poor buried hopes come up together
  And overcharge my spirits. I am weak.
  Some say (however ill) the sea and women
  Are governed by the moon: both ebb and flow,
  Both full of changes. Yet to them that know
  And truly judge, these but opinions are,
  And heresies to bring on pleasing war
  Between our tempers, that without these were

50

55

60

---

38 *kind* natural – in this context fickle, disloyal
43 *Dissemble it* Pretend
44 *heavy mace* the traditional emblem of Morpheus, god of sleep
45 *heavy* drowsy
47 *distempers* mental or physical disorders
50 *ravished* transported (from the body)
54 *She is only* She alone is
62–6 *opinions ... Cupid* empty and false notions that pleasantly disturb the balance of our emotions; for without these we should experience neither love in retrospect nor the pangs of anxiety which are love's chief joys

Both void of after-love and present fear   65
Which are the best of Cupid. Oh thou child
Bred from despair, I dare not entertain thee,
Having a love without the faults of women,
And greater in her perfect goods than men;
Which to make good, and please myself the stronger,   70
Though certainly I am certain of her love,
I'll try her, that the world and memory
May sing to aftertimes her constancy.

A test

                                   [*Draws his sword*]

Luce, Luce, awake.
LUCE   Why do you fright me, friend,
With those distempered looks? What makes your sword   75
Drawn in your hand! Who hath offended you?
I prithee, Jasper, sleep; thou art wild with watching.
JASPER
Come, make your way to heaven, and bid the world
(With all the villainies that stick upon it)
Farewell; you're for another life.
LUCE   Oh Jasper,   80
How have my tender years committed evil
(Especially against the man I love)
Thus to be cropped untimely?
JASPER   Foolish girl,
Canst thou imagine I could love his daughter,
That flung me from my fortune into nothing,   85
Discharged me his service, shut the doors
Upon my poverty, and scorned my prayers,
Sending me, like a boat without a mast,
To sink or swim? Come, by this hand you die;
I must have life and blood to satisfy   90
Your father's wrongs.

WIFE
Away, George, away; raise the watch at Ludgate, and bring
a mittimus from the justice for this desperate villain! – Now

---

66 *child* i.e. mistrust
70 *make good* demonstrate
72 *try* put to the test
75 ff. In Beaumont and Fletcher's later plays maidens have a distressing habit of being wounded by their own lovers' swords.
90 *satisfy* compensate
92 *Ludgate* Like Newgate, it was used as a prison and a station for the watch.
93 *mittimus* warrant for arrest (<Latin 'we send', the first word of the writ)

I charge you, gentlemen, see the king's peace kept! – Oh,
my heart, what a varlet's this to offer manslaughter upon   95
the harmless gentlewoman!

CITIZEN

I warrant thee, sweetheart, we'll have him hampered.

LUCE   Oh, Jasper, be not cruel;
If thou wilt kill me, smile and do it quickly,
And let not many deaths appear before me.   100
I am a woman made of fear and love,
A weak, weak woman; kill not with thy eyes,
They shoot me through and through. Strike, I am ready;
And, dying, still I love thee.

Enter MERCHANT, HUMPHREY, *and his men*

MERCHANT   Whereabouts?

JASPER [*Aside*]
No more of this, now to myself again.   105

HUMPHREY

There, there he stands with sword, like martial knight,
Drawn in his hand; therefore beware the fight,
You that be wise; for, were I good Sir Bevis,
I would not stay his coming, by your leaves.

MERCHANT

Sirrah, restore my daughter.

JASPER   Sirrah, no.   110

MERCHANT

Upon him, then!

[*The servants attack and wound* JASPER]

WIFE

So, down with him, down with him, down with him! Cut
him i'th' leg, boys, cut him i'th' leg!

MERCHANT

Come your ways, minion. I'll provide a cage
                         hussy

97 *hampered* confined
100 *many deaths* Compare 'Cowards die many times before their deaths' (*Julius Caesar*, II.ii.32).
104 *Whereabouts?* The incongruity of Venturewell's 'reply' to Luce's declamation is intentional.
108 *Sir Bevis* the hero of 'Sir Bevis of Hampton', a famous medieval romance
109 *stay* await
114 *minion* hussy

For you, you're grown so tame. – Horse her away!   115

HUMPHREY

Truly I'm glad your forces have the day.

Exeunt, manet JASPER

JASPER

They are gone, and I am hurt; my love is lost,
Never to get again. Oh, me unhappy,
Bleed, bleed, and die! I cannot. Oh my folly,
Thou hast betrayed me! Hope, where art thou fled?   120
Tell me if thou be'st anywhere remaining.
Shall I but see my love again? Oh, no!
She will not deign to look upon her butcher,
Nor is it fit she should; yet I must venture.
Oh, chance, or fortune, or whate'er thou art   125
That men adore for powerful, hear my cry,
And let me loving live, or losing die!   *Exit*

WIFE

Is 'a gone, George?

CITIZEN

Ay, cony.

WIFE

Marry, and let him go, sweetheart. By the faith o' my body,   130
'a has put me into such a fright that I tremble, as they say,
as 'twere an aspen leaf. Look o' my little finger, George,
how it shakes. Now, i'truth, every member of my body is
the worse for't.

CITIZEN

Come, hug in mine arms, sweet mouse; he shall not fright   135
thee any more. Alas, mine own dear heart, how it quivers.

Enter MISTRESS MERRYTHOUGHT, RAFE, MICHAEL, [TIM
as] *Squire,* [GEORGE *as*] *Dwarf,* HOST, *and a* TAPSTER

WIFE

Oh, Rafe, how dost thou, Rafe? How hast thou slept
tonight? Has the knight used thee well?

CITIZEN

Peace, Nell; let Rafe alone.

115 *tame* (sexually) submissive
118 *unhappy* troublesome
126 *for* as
138 *tonight* last night

TAPSTER

Master, the reckoning is not paid.   140

RAFE

Right courteous knight, who, for the order's sake
Which thou hast ta'en, hang'st out the holy bell,
As I this flaming pestle bear about,
We render thanks to your puissant self,
Your beauteous lady, and your gentle squires,   145
For thus refreshing of our wearied limbs,
Stiffened with hard achievements in wild desert.

TAPSTER

Sir, there is twelve shillings to pay.

RAFE

Thou merry squire Tapstero, thanks to thee
For comforting our souls with double jug;   150
And if advent'rous fortune prick thee forth,
Thou jovial squire, to follow feats of arms,
Take heed thou tender every lady's cause,
Every true knight, and every damsel fair;
But spill the blood of treacherous Saracens   155
And false enchanters that with magic spells
Have done to death full many a noble knight.

HOST

Thou valiant Knight of the Burning Pestle, give ear to me:
there is twelve shillings to pay, and as I am a true knight, I
will not bate a penny.   160

WIFE

George, I pray thee tell me: must Rafe pay twelve shillings
now?

CITIZEN

No, Nell, no; nothing but the old knight is merry with Rafe.

WIFE

Oh, is't nothing else? Rafe will be as merry as he.

140 *reckoning* bill
148 *twelve shillings* the bill is not exorbitant
150 *double jug* strong ale
151 *advent'rous* hazardous
    prick thee forth spur you on
153 *tender* support
154 *Every true ... fair* Q2 (Euery truery true Knight, and euery damsell faire faire Q1)
155 *Saracens* The Mahommedan enemies of the Crusaders; but the description is applied loosely to the villains of the romances.
160 *bate* deduct

RAFE
Sir knight, this mirth of yours becomes you well;   165
But to requite this liberal courtesy,
If any of your squires will follow arms,
He shall receive from my heroic hand
A knighthood, by the virtue of this pestle.
HOST
Fair knight, I thank you for your noble offer;   170
Therefore, gentle knight,
Twelve shillings you must pay, or I must cap you.

WIFE
Look, George, did not I tell thee as much; the Knight of the
Bell is in earnest. Rafe shall not be beholding to him; give
him his money, George, and let him go snick up.   175
CITIZEN
Cap Rafe? No. – Hold your hand, Sir Knight of the Bell;
there's your money. Have you anything to say to Rafe now?
Cap Rafe!
WIFE
I would you should know it, Rafe has friends that will not
suffer him to be capped for ten times so much, and ten   180
times to the end of that. – Now take thy course, Rafe.

MISTRESS MERRYTHOUGHT
Come, Michael, thou and I will go home to thy father; he
hath enough left to keep us a day or two, and we'll set
fellows abroad to cry our purse and our casket. Shall we,
Michael?   185
MICHAEL
Ay, I pray, mother. In truth my feet are full of chilblains
with travelling.

WIFE
Faith, and those chilblains are a foul trouble. Mistress
Merrythought, when your youth comes home, let him rub
all the soles of his feet and the heels and his ankles with a   190
mouse skin; or, if none of your people can catch a mouse,
when he goes to bed let him roll his feet in the warm
embers, and I warrant you he shall be well; and you may

171 The sense is incomplete and presumably some words have dropped out.
172 *cap* seize, arrest
174 *beholding* vulgarism for 'beholden'
181 *to ... of* in addition to
184 *cry* announce the loss of

make him put his fingers between his toes and smell to
them; it's very sovereign for his head if he be costive.   195

MISTRESS MERRYTHOUGHT
Master Knight of the Burning Pestle, my son Michael and I
bid you farewell; I thank your worship heartily for your
kindness.
RAFE
Farewell, fair lady, and your tender squire.
If, pricking through these deserts, I do hear   200
Of any traitorous knight who through his guile
Hath light upon your casket and your purse,
I will despoil him of them and restore them.
MISTRESS MERRYTHOUGHT
I thank your worship.

Exit with MICHAEL

RAFE
Dwarf, bear my shield; squire, elevate my lance;   205
And now farewell, you Knight of Holy Bell.

CITIZEN
Ay, ay, Rafe, all is paid.

RAFE
But yet before I go, speak, worthy knight,
If aught you do of sad adventures know,
Where errant knight may through his prowess win   210
Eternal fame, and free some gentle souls
From endless bonds of steel and ling'ring pain.
HOST [*to* TAPSTER]
Sirrah, go to Nick the barber, and bid him prepare himself
as I told you before, quickly.
TAPSTER
I am gone, sir.   *Exit* TAPSTER   215
HOST
Sir knight, this wilderness affordeth none
But the great venture where full many a knight
Hath tried his prowess and come off with shame,
And where I would not have you lose your life

195 *sovereign* good
    costive constipated
209 *sad* grave
210 *knight* ed. (knights Q1)
213 *Nick* Don Quixote's barber was called Master Nicholas (I.v).

Against no man, but furious fiend of hell. 220
RAFE
  Speak on, sir knight, tell what he is and where;
  For here I vow upon my blazing badge,
  Never to blaze a day in quietness;
  But bread and water will I only eat,
  And the green herb and rock shall be my couch, 225
  Till I have quelled that man or beast or fiend
  That works such damage to all errant knights.
HOST
  Not far from hence, near to a craggy cliff,
  At the north end of this distressèd town,
  There doth stand a lowly house 230
  Ruggedly builded, and in it a cave
  In which an ugly giant now doth won,
  Yclepèd Barbaroso. In his hand
  He shakes a naked lance of purest steel,
  With sleeves turned up, and him before he wears 235
  A motley garment to preserve his clothes
  From blood of those knights which he massacres,
  And ladies gent. Without his door doth hang
  A copper basin on a prickant spear,
  At which no sooner gentle knights can knock 240
  But the shrill sound fierce Barbaroso hears,
  And, rushing forth, brings in the errant knight,
  And sets him down in an enchanted chair.   ·
  Then with an engine which he hath prepared,
  With forty teeth, he claws his courtly crown; 245
  Next makes him wink, and underneath his chin

223 *blaze* probably caught from 'blazing' above, although it could mean 'burn with devotion'; Dyce conjectured 'lose' or 'pass'
226 *quelled* slain
232 *ugly* fearsome
    won dwell
233 *Yclepèd* Named
    Barbaroso for Barbarossa (see III, 324), the name for Frederick I of Germany (1123–90)
238 *gent* noble, fair
239 *copper basin on a prickant spear* The sign of the barber-surgeon; the pole was painted red and white and, together with the basin, signified that the barber not only cut hair but drew teeth and let blood.
    prickant pointing upward
240 *can* do
246 *wink* For the purpose of anointing his eyes with perfumed water, see III, 379.

He plants a brazen pece of mighty bord,
And knocks his bullets round about his cheeks,
Whilst, with his fingers and an instrument
With which he snaps his hair off, he doth fill   250
The wretch's ears with a most hideous noise.
Thus every knight adventurer he doth trim,
And now no creature dares encounter him.

RAFE

In God's name, I will fight with him. Kind sir,
Go but before me to this dismal cave   255
Where this huge giant Barbaroso dwells,
And, by that virtue that brave Rosicleer
That damnèd brood of ugly giants slew,
And Palmerin Frannarco overthrew,
I doubt not but to curb this traitor foul,   260
And to the devil send his guilty soul.

HOST

Brave sprighted knight, thus far I will perform
This your request: I'll bring you within sight
Of this most loathsome place, inhabited
By a more loathsome man; but dare not stay,   265
For his main force swoops all he sees away.

RAFE

Saint George, set on before! March, squire and page.

Exeunt

247 *pece* cup
   bord rim
248 *bullets* small balls of soap
250 *snaps his hair off* The long hair affected by gallants was often satirized – see III, 378 below; Beaumont's *The Woman Hater*, V.iv.165; Dekker's *Gull's Hornbook,* Ch. iii; and Stubbes, i. 67–9
252 *trim* often used figuratively meaning to thrash or trounce
254 *with* Q2 (om. Q1)
257 *virtue that* virtue with which; 'that' is to be understood again before 'Palmerin' in l. 259
258 *damnèd ... giants* Rafe has in mind Rosicleer's adventure with the giant Brandagedeon and his thirty knights, told in *The Mirror of Knighthood*, I. xxxvi (Murch).
259 *Frannarco* The account of how Palmerin slew the giant Frannarco is found in *Palmerin d'Oliva*, I. li – the chapter from which Rafe read in I, 214 ff.
266 *main* full, sheer
   swoops Q2 (soopes Q1)
267 *St George* Redolent of nostalgia for a chivalric dream; compare 'Saint George that swinged the dragon, and e'er since / Sits on's horseback at mine hostess' door' (*King John*, II.ii.288–9).

WIFE

George, dost think Rafe will confound the giant?

CITIZEN

I hold my cap to a farthing he does. Why, Nell, I saw him
wrestle with the great Dutchman and hurl him.   270

WIFE

Faith, and that Dutchman was a goodly man, if all things
were answerable to his bigness; and yet they say there was
a Scotchman higher than he, and that they two and a knight
met and saw one another for nothing; but of all the sights
that ever were in London since I was married, methinks the   275
little child that was so fair grown about the members was
the prettiest, that and the hermaphrodite.

CITIZEN

Nay, by your leave, Nell, Ninivie was better.

WIFE

Ninivie? Oh, that was the story of Joan and the wall, was
it not, George?   280

CITIZEN

Yes, lamb.

Enter MISTRESS MERRYTHOUGHT

WIFE

Look, George, here comes Mistress Merrythought again,
and I would have Rafe come and fight with the giant. I tell
you true, I long to see't.

CITIZEN

Good Mistress Merrythought, begone, I pray you, for my   285
sake. I pray you, forbear a little; you shall have audience
presently; I have a little business.

WIFE

Mistress Merrythought, if it please you to refrain your

---

270 *Dutchman* For the Elizabethans 'Dutchmen' included speakers of both High and
    Low German. It is impossible to identify for certain whom the Wife refers to –
    Sugden gives references to a huge German fencer who lived in London (pp. 164
    and 221); see also Murch, p. 199.

272 *bigness* the size of his member

276 *little child* Like Jonson, Beaumont is satirising the citizens' taste for freaks – cf.
    Jonson, *The Alchemist*, V.i.21 ff.

278 *Ninivie* 'Nineveh, with Jonas and the Whale' was an extremely popular motion
    (puppet play) of the time (Jonah preached in Nineveh after escaping from the
    whale).

279 *Joan* proverbially promiscuous ('Joan is as good as my lady in the dark'; Tilley
    J57)

passion a little till Rafe have dispatched the giant out of the
way, we shall think ourselves much bound to you. I thank   290
you, good Mistress Merrythought.

Exit MISTRESS MERRYTHOUGHT

Enter a BOY

CITIZEN

Boy, come hither; send away Rafe and this whoreson giant
quickly.

BOY

In good faith, sir, we cannot. You'll utterly spoil our play,
and make it to be hissed, and it cost money; you will not   295
suffer us to go on with our plot. – I pray, gentlemen, rule
him.

CITIZEN

Let him come now and dispatch this, and I'll trouble you no
more.

BOY

Will you give me your hand of that?   300

WIFE

Give him thy hand, George, do, and I'll kiss him. I warrant
thee the youth means plainly.

BOY

I'll send him to you presently.   *Exit* BOY

WIFE

I thank you, little youth. – Faith, the child hath a sweet
breath, George, but I think it be troubled with the worms.   305
Carduus benedictus and mare's milk were the only thing in
the world for't.

> *Enter* RAFE, HOST, [TIM *as*] *Squire, and* [GEORGE *as*]
> *Dwarf*

Oh, Rafe's here, George. – God send thee good luck, Rafe.

HOST

Puissant knight, yonder his mansion is;
Lo, where the spear and copper basin are;   310

289 *dispatched* Q2 (dispatch Q1)
292 *away* along
302 *plainly* honestly
303 *presently* immediately
306 *Carduus benedictus* the blessed thistle, used as a panacea
    mare's milk Mare's milk was considered useful for purging (Murch).
307 s.d. *ed.* (after l. 308 Q1)

Behold that string on which hangs many a tooth
Drawn from the gentle jaw of wandering knights.
I dare not stay to sound; he will appear.   *Exit* HOST
RAFE
Oh, faint not, heart! Susan, my lady dear,
The cobbler's maid in Milk Street, for whose sake   315
I take these arms, oh let the thought of thee
Carry thy knight through all adventurous deeds,
And in the honour of thy beauteous self
May I destroy this monster Barbaroso. –
Knock, squire, upon the basin till it break   320
With the shrill strokes, or till the giant speak.

[TIM *knocks*]

Enter BARBER

WIFE
Oh, George, the giant, the giant! – Now, Rafe, for thy life!

BARBER
What fond unknowing wight is this that dares
So rudely knock at Barbaroso's cell,
Where no man comes but leaves his fleece behind!   325
RAFE
I, traitorous caitiff, who am sent by fate
To punish all the sad enormities
Thou hast committed against ladies gent
And errant knights. Traitor to God and men,
Prepare thyself; this is the dismal hour   330
Appointed for thee to give strict account
Of all thy beastly treacherous villainies.
BARBER
Foolhardy knight, full soon thou shalt aby

---

313 *sound* blow a horn
314 ff. The incidents in this contest, the invocation of the lady (Susan is the equivalent of Don Quixote's Dulcinea), the formal challenge, the hero's magnanimity, etc., are parodies of conventions in the romances.
315 *Milk Street* ran north from Cheapside
323 *fond* foolish
      wight man
325 *fleece* pun meaning hair and money (cf. 'to fleece someone')
326 *caitiff* wretch, rogue
333 *aby* pay for

He takes down his pole

This fond reproach: thy body will I bang,
And, lo, upon that string thy teeth shall hang.   335
Prepare thyself, for dead soon shalt thou be.

RAFE
Saint George for me!

BARBER
Gargantua for me!

They fight

WIFE
To him, Rafe, to him! Hold up the giant; set out thy leg
before, Rafe.   340

CITIZEN
Falsify a blow, Rafe; falsify a blow; the giant lies open on
the left side.

WIFE
Bear't off; bear't off still. There, boy. – Oh, Rafe's almost
down, Rafe's almost down.

RAFE
Susan, inspire me! – Now have up again.   345

WIFE
Up, up, up, up, up! So, Rafe, down with him, down with
him, Rafe.

CITIZEN
Fetch him o'er the hip, boy.

WIFE
There, boy; kill, kill, kill, kill, kill, Rafe.

CITIZEN
No, Rafe, get all out of him first.   350

[RAFE *knocks the* BARBER *down*]

335 *string* Drawn teeth were hung on a string outside the barber's shop; cf. *The
      Woman Hater*, III.iii.109–10.
338 *Gargantua* more probably the hero of the folk-tale than of Rabelais' work which
      was little known in England at this date – see *Every Man in his Humour* (1616),
      III.ii.25, and Huntingdon Brown, *Rabelais in English Literature*, (Cambridge,
      Mass., 1933)
338 s.d. Q1 prints on line 337
341 *Falsify* Feign
343 *Bear* Fend

RAFE
  Presumptuous man, see to what desperate end
  Thy treachery hath brought thee. The just gods,
  Who never prosper those that do despise them,
  For all the villainies which thou hast done
  To knights and ladies, now have paid thee home   355
  By my stiff arm, a knight adventurous.
  But say, vile wretch, before I send thy soul
  To sad Avernus, whither it must go,
  What captives hold'st thou in thy sable cave?
BARBER
  Go in and free them all; thou hast the day.   360
RAFE
  Go, squire and dwarf, search in this dreadful cave,
  And free the wretched prisoners from their bonds.

          Exeunt [TIM *as*] *Squire and* [GEORGE *as*] *Dwarf*

BARBER
  I crave for mercy, as thou art a knight,
  And scorn'st to spill the blood of those that beg.
RAFE
  Thou show'd'st no mercy, nor shalt thou have any;   365
  Prepare thyself, for thou shalt surely die.

          Enter [TIM *as*] *Squire leading one winking, with a
                    basin under his chin*

TIM
  Behold, brave knight, here is one prisoner,
  Whom this wild man hath usèd as you see.

WIFE
  This is the first wise word I heard the squire speak.

RAFE
  Speak what thou art, and how thou hast been used,   370
  That I may give him condign punishment.

---

355 *paid ... home* fully punished
358 *Avernus* Lake Avernus, near Naples; its gloomy appearance gave rise to the
    belief that it was an entrance to the underworld
359 *sable* black
366 s.d 1 *winking* with his eyes shut
371 *That ... condign* Q2 (That that I may giue condigne Q1)
    condign appropriate

1 KNIGHT

    I am a knight that took my journey post
    Northward from London, and in courteous wise
    This giant trained me to his loathsome den
    Under pretence of killing of the itch;   375
    And all my body with a powder strewed,
    That smarts and stings, and cut away my beard
    And my curled locks wherein were ribands tied,
    And with a water washed my tender eyes
    (Whilst up and down about me still he skipped),   380
    Whose virtue is, that till mine eyes be wiped
    With a dry cloth, for this my foul disgrace
    I shall not dare to look a dog i'th' face.

WIFE

    Alas, poor knight. – Relieve him, Rafe; relieve poor knights
    whilst you live.   385

RAFE

    My trusty squire, convey him to the town,
    Where he may find relief. – Adieu, fair knight.

        Exit KNIGHT [*with* TIM, *who presently re-enters*]

        Enter [GEORGE *as*] *Dwarf leading one*
          with a patch o'er his nose

GEORGE

    Puissant Knight of the Burning Pestle hight,
    See here another wretch, whom this foul beast
    Hath scorched and scored in this inhuman wise.   390

RAFE

    Speak me thy name and eke thy place of birth,
    And what hath been thy usage in this cave.

2 KNIGHT

    I am a knight, Sir Pockhole is my name,
    And by my birth I am a Londoner,

---

372 *post* in haste

374 *trained* lured

375 *itch* the result of sexual excess; cf. *The Wild-Goose Chase*, I.i: 'They cannot rub
    off old friends, their French itches.'

378 *ribands* ribbons

387 s.d. *patch … nose* He is suffering from an advanced stage of the French pox or
    syphilis that eventually attacks the bones.

390 *scorched* slashed with a knife (to empty the syphilitic sores)

Free by my copy; but my ancestors   395
Were Frenchmen all; and riding hard this way
Upon a trotting horse, my bones did ache;
And I, faint knight, to ease my weary limbs,
Light at this cave, when straight this furious fiend,
With sharpest instrument of purest steel   400
Did cut the gristle of my nose away,
And in the place this velvet plaster stands.
Relieve me, gentle knight, out of his hands.

WIFE
Good Rafe, relieve Sir Pockhole and send him away, for,
in truth, his breath stinks.   405

RAFE
Convey him straight after the other knight. –
Sir Pockhole, fare you well.
2 KNIGHT   Kind sir, goodnight.

Exit [KNIGHT *with* GEORGE, *who presently re-enters*]

Cries within

3 KNIGHT
Deliver us!
WOMAN
Deliver us!

WIFE
Hark, George, what a woeful cry there is. I think some   410
woman lies in there.

3 KNIGHT
Deliver us!
WOMAN
Deliver us!
RAFE
What ghastly noise is this? Speak, Barbaroso,
Or by this blazing steel thy head goes off.   415

---

395 *copy* certificate of admission to the freedom of the City
397 *trotting horse* i.e. a whore
402 *velvet plaster* Velvet patches were used to cover both honourable scars and the
     incisions made to relieve venereal disease; cf. *All's Well*, IV.v.85.
411 *lies in* is giving birth
412 s.p. *3 KNIGHT* Throughout the scene, the Third Knight's speeches are prefixed
     MAN in Q1–3, F.

BARBER

Prisoners of mine, whom I in diet keep.
Send lower down into the cave,
And in a tub that's heated smoking hot,
There may they find them and deliver them.

RAFE

Run, squire and dwarf, deliver them with speed. 420

Exeunt [TIM *as*] *Squire and* [GEORGE *as*] *Dwarf*

WIFE

But will not Rafe kill this giant? Surely I am afeared if he
let him go he will do as much hurt as ever he did.

CITIZEN

Not so, mouse, neither, if he could convert him.

WIFE

Ay, George, if he could convert him; but a giant is not so
soon converted as one of us ordinary people. There's a 425
pretty tale of a witch that had the devil's mark about her,
God bless us, that had a giant to her son, that was called
Lob-lie-by-the-fire; didst never hear it, George?

Enter [TIM *as*] *Squire leading a man with a glass of
lotion in his hand, and* [GEORGE *as*] *Dwarf leading a
woman with diet-bread and drink*

CITIZEN

Peace, Nell, here comes the prisoners.

GEORGE

Here be these pinèd wretches, manful knight, 430
That for these six weeks have not seen a wight.

RAFE

Deliver what you are, and how you came
To this sad cave, and what your usage was.

3 KNIGHT

I am an errant knight that followed arms

---

418 *tub* Sweating-tubs were used as a cure for the pox; cf. *Timon of Athens*, IV.iii.86.
423 *convert* The conversion of enemies was a romance theme.
426 *devil's mark* Witches were supposed to be branded by the devil.
428 *Lob-lie-by-the-fire* Little is known of this creature – see J. H. Ewing, *Lob-lie-by-the-fire* (London, 1937) and cf. *The Faerie Queene*, III.vii.12, the canto in which the Squire of Dames (see II, 169 n.) also appears.
428 s.d. 3 *diet-bread* special bread for syphilitics
430 *pinèd* starved, wasted
432 *Deliver* State

With spear and shield, and in my tender years   435
I stricken was with Cupid's fiery shaft
And fell in love with this my lady dear,
And stole her from her friends in Turnbull Street,
And bore her up and down from town to town
Where we did eat and drink and music hear,   440
Till at the length, at this unhappy town
We did arrive, and coming to this cave,
This beast us caught and put us in a tub
Where we this two months sweat, and should have done
Another month if you had not relieved us.   445

WOMAN
This bread and water hath our diet been,
Together with a rib cut from a neck
Of burnèd mutton; hard hath been our fare.
Release us from this ugly giant's snare.

3 KNIGHT
This hath been all the food we have received;   450
But only twice a day, for novelty,
He gave a spoonful of this hearty broth

                              Pulls out a syringe

To each of us, through this same slender quill.

RAFE
From this infernal monster you shall go,
That useth knights and gentle ladies so. –   455
Convey them hence.

        Exeunt [3 KNIGHT] *and woman* [*with* TIM *and* GEORGE
                                who presently re-enter]

CITIZEN
Cony, I can tell thee the gentlemen like Rafe.

WIFE
Ay, George, I see it well enough. – Gentlemen, I thank you
all heartily for gracing my man Rafe, and I promise you you
shall see him oft'ner.   460

BARBER
Mercy, great knight, I do recant my ill,

438 *Turnbull Street* Originally Turnmill Street, it runs south from Clerkenwell
    Green. It was a notorious haunt of prostitutes, cf. *2 Henry IV*, III.ii.295.
441 *at the length* at length (Abbott, 91)
452 *hearty* strengthening
453 *slender quill* probably a clyster-pipe (enema-pump)

And henceforth never gentle blood will spill.
RAFE
I give thee mercy; but yet shalt thou swear
Upon my burning pestle to perform
Thy promise utterèd.   465
BARBER
I swear and kiss. *[kisses the pestle]*
RAFE   Depart then, and amend.

[Exit BARBER]

– Come, squire and dwarf, the sun grows towards his set,
And we have many more adventures yet.

Exeunt

CITIZEN
Now Rafe is in this humour, I know he would ha' beaten
all the boys in the house if they had been set on him.   470
WIFE
Ay, George, but it is well as it is; I warrant you the
gentlemen do consider what it is to overthrow a giant.

Enter MISTRESS MERRYTHOUGHT *and* MICHAEL

But look, George, here comes Mistress Merrythought and
her son Michael. – Now you are welcome, Mistress
Merrythought, now Rafe has done, you may go on.   475

MISTRESS MERRYTHOUGHT
Mick, my boy.
MICHAEL
Ay, forsooth, mother.
MISTRESS MERRYTHOUGHT
Be merry, Mick; we are at home now, where, I warrant
you, you shall find the house flung out at the windows.

[Music within]

Hark, hey dogs, hey; this is the old world, i'faith, with my   480
husband. If I get in among 'em, I'll play 'em such a lesson
that they shall have little list to come scraping hither again.

472 s.d. ed. (after 475 Q1)
479 *the house ... windows* a scene of roisterous merry-making (Tilley H785)
480 *Hark, hey dogs, hey* 'Listen to them yapping' (Zitner) .
      world habit
482 *scraping* fiddling

– Why, Master Merrythought, husband, Charles Merrythought!

OLD MERRYTHOUGHT ([*sings*] *within*)

> *If you will sing and dance and laugh,*   485
>   *And hollo and laugh again,*
> *And then cry, 'There, boys, there', why then*
>   *One, two, three, and four,*
>   *We shall be merry within this hour.*

MISTRESS MERRYTHOUGHT

Why, Charles, do you not know your own natural wife? I   490
say, open the door, and turn me out those mangy
companions; 'tis more than time that they were fellow and
fellow like with you. You are a gentleman, Charles, and an
old man, and father of two children; and I myself (though I
say it) by my mother's side niece to a worshipful gentleman,   495
and a conductor; he has been three times in his majesty's
service at Chester, and is now the fourth time, God bless
him and his charge, upon his journey.

OLD MERRYTHOUGHT [*sings within*]

> *Go from my window, love, go;*
> *Go from my window, my dear;*   500
>   *The wind and the rain*
>   *Will drive you back again;*
>   *You cannot be lodgèd here.*

Hark you, Mistress Merrythought, you that walk upon   *A man*
adventures and forsake your husband because he sings with   *that knows*   505
never a penny in his purse; what, shall I think myself the   *his worth*
worse? Faith, no, I'll be merry. You come not here; here's

---

485 s.d. *within* Merrythought may have appeared at the window stage above (see ll.
    499 & 565; cf. Smith, pp. 375 ff.)

485–9 'a recitative improvisation' (Zitner)

486 *hollo* shout

491 *me* ethical dative (Abbott, 220)

492 *companions* rascals

492–3 '*tis ... you* they have kept you company for far too long

495 *worshipful* honourable

496 *conductor* captain

497 *Chester* a notorious centre for military corruption (see C. G. Cruickshank,
    Elizabeth's Army, (Oxford, 1966), pp. 139–41

499 ff. and 518 ff. *Go ... here* a popular song that appears also in *Monsieur
    Thomas*, III.iii, *The Woman's Prize*, I.iii, and Heywood's *The Rape of Lucrece*;
    music in Simpson, pp. 257–9 and Poulton, pp. 165–7; see also Baskervill, pp.
    450–64

none but lads of mettle, lives of a hundred years and
upwards; care never drunk their bloods, nor want made
'em warble, [*sings*]   510
   Heigh-ho, my heart is heavy.
MISTRESS MERRYTHOUGHT
Why, Master Merrythought, what am I that you should
laugh me to scorn thus abruptly! Am I not your fellow-
feeler, as we may say, in all our miseries, your comforter in
health and sickness? Have I not brought you children! Are   515
they not like you, Charles? Look upon thine own image,
hard-hearted man. And yet for all this –
OLD MERRYTHOUGHT ([*sings*] *within*)
   Begone, begone, my Juggy, my puggy,
   Begone, my love, my dear.
     The weather is warm   520
     'Twill do thee no harm
   Thou canst not be lodgèd here.
– Be merry, boys; some light music, and more wine!

WIFE
He's not in earnest, I hope, George, is he?
CITIZEN
What if he be, sweetheart?   525
WIFE
Marry, if he be, George, I'll make bold to tell him he's an
ingrant old man to use his bed-fellow so scurvily.
CITIZEN
What, how does he use her, honey?
WIFE
Marry come up, Sir Saucebox, I think you'll take his part,
will you not? Lord, how hot you are grown. You are a fine   530
man, an you had a fine dog; it becomes you sweetly.
CITIZEN
Nay, prithee, Nell, chide not. For as I am an honest man
and a true Christian grocer, I do not like his doings.

508–9 *lives ... upwards* their merry lives have kept them young
513–14 *fellow-feeler* a nonce word
518 *Juggy* diminutive of Joan
    puggy term of endearment
526 *Marry* Indeed
527 *ingrant* ignorant, ill-mannered
529 *Marry come up* a taunt = 'Now, now'
530–31 *You ... dog* 'You are not the stud you think you are'.

WIFE

I cry you mercy then, George. You know we are all frail
and full of infirmities. – D'ye hear, Master Merrythought,   535
may I crave a word with you?

OLD MERRYTHOUGHT (*within*)

Strike up lively, lads.

WIFE

I had not thought, in truth, Master Merrythought, that a
man of your age and discretion, as I may say, being a
gentleman, and therefore known by your gentle conditions,   540
could have used so little respect to the weakness of his wife.
For your wife is your own flesh, the staff of your age, your
yoke-fellow, with whose help you draw through the mire of
this transitory world. Nay, she's your own rib. And again –

OLD MERRYTHOUGHT ([*sings*] *within*)

> I come not hither for thee to teach,   545
> I have no pulpit for thee to preach,
> I would thou hadst kissed me under the breech,
> As thou art a lady gay.

WIFE

Marry, with a vengeance! I am heartily sorry for the poor
gentlewoman. – But if I were thy wife, I'faith, grey-beard,   550
i'faith –

CITIZEN

I prithee, sweet honeysuckle, be content.

WIFE

Give me such words that am a gentlewoman born! Hang
him, hoary rascal! Get me some drink, George, I am almost
molten with fretting: now beshrew his knave's heart for it.   555

[*Exit* CITIZEN]

OLD MERRYTHOUGHT [*within*]

Play me a light lavolta. Come, be frolic. Fill the good fellows' wine.

---

534 *cry you mercy* beg your pardon
540 *conditions* qualities
543 *yoke-fellow* (literally) companion at the plough
556 *lavolta* a lively dance for two people
    frolic merry

MISTRESS MERRYTHOUGHT

Why, Master Merrythought, are you disposed to make me
wait here? You'll open, I hope; I'll fetch them that shall
open else.   560

OLD MERRYTHOUGHT [*within*]

Good woman, if you will sing I'll give you something; if
not –

Song

> *You are no love for me, Marg'ret,*
> *I am no love for you.*

Come aloft, boys, aloft.   565

MISTRESS MERRYTHOUGHT

Now a churl's fart in your teeth, sir. – Come, Mick, we'll
not trouble him; 'a shall not ding us i'th'teeth with his
bread and his broth, that he shall not. Come, boy; I'll
provide for thee, I warrant thee. We'll go to Master
Venturewell's, the merchant; I'll get his letter to mine host 570
of the Bell in Waltham; there I'll place thee with the tapster.
Will not that do well for thee, Mick? And let me alone for
that old cuckoldly knave your father; I'll use him in his
kind, I warrant ye.

[*Exeunt*]

Finis Actus tertii

563–4 *You ... you* probably a fragment of some version of the ballad of Fair
    Margaret and Sweet William – see II, 431n.

565 *Come ... aloft* (printed as part of preceding song in Q1–3, F) 'The expression is
    generally found applied to apes that were taught to vault: here it is used merely
    as an incitement to mirth' (Dyce).

567 *ding* strike, i.e. taunt

567–8 *with ... broth* for supporting us

572 *for* to deal with (Abbott, 147)

573–4 *in his kind* as he deserves

574 s.d. 2 *Finis ... Music* printed below line 6 of following interlude in Q1–3, F

[Interlude III]

Music [Enter BOY]

[*Enter* CITIZEN]

WIFE

Come, George, where's the beer?

CITIZEN

Here, love.

WIFE

This old fornicating fellow will not out of my mind yet. –
Gentlemen, I'll begin to you all, and I desire more of your
acquaintance, with all my heart. [*Drinks*] Fill the gentlemen   5
some beer, George.

BOY *danceth*

Look, George, the little boy's come again; methinks he
looks something like the Prince of Orange in his long
stocking, if he had a little harness about his neck. George, I
will have him dance 'Fading'. – 'Fading' is a fine jig, I'll   10
assure you, gentlemen. – Begin, brother. – Now 'a capers,
sweetheart. – Now a turn o'th'toe, and then tumble.
Cannot you tumble, youth?

BOY

No, indeed, forsooth.

WIFE

Nor eat fire?   15

BOY

Neither.

WIFE

Why then, I thank you heartily. There's twopence to buy
you points withal.

[*Exit* BOY]

---

4 *begin to* toast

8 *Prince of Orange* probably a reference to a well-known picture of Prince
Maurice, son of William of Orange

9 *harness* armour

10 '*Fading*' an Irish country dance (music in Simpson, pp. 792–5), also copulation
(Partridge, pp. 101–2)

12 *tumble* for the popularity of 'antic dances' and tumbling in the playhouses,
see Baskervill, pp. 95, 145n., and 367–8

18 *points* tagged laces for tying hose to doublet

Act IV

Enter JASPER *and* [*a*] BOY

JASPER [*gives a letter*]
  There, boy, deliver this, but do it well.
  Hast thou provided me four lusty fellows
  Able to carry me? And art thou perfect
  In all thy business?
BOY   Sir, you need not fear:
  I have my lesson here and cannot miss it.   5
  The men are ready for you, and what else
  Pertains to this employment.
JASPER [*gives him money*]   There, my boy;
  Take it, but buy no land.
BOY   Faith, sir, 'twere rare
  To see so young a purchaser. I fly,
  And on my wings carry your destiny.   *Exit*   10
JASPER
  Go, and be happy. – Now, my latest hope,
  Forsake me not, but fling thy anchor out
  And let it hold. Stand fixed, thou rolling stone,
  Till I enjoy my dearest. Hear me, all
  You powers that rule in men celestial.   *Exit*   15

WIFE
Go thy ways; thou art as crooked a sprig as ever grew in
London. I warrant him, he'll come to some naughty end or
other, for his looks say no less. Besides, his father (you
know, George) is none of the best; you heard him take me

Act IV ed. (Q1–3, F print 'Actus Quartus, Scoena prima' above s.d. 'BOY
    danceth' of the preceding interlude)

  1–2 printed as prose in Q1

  2 *four* see 231 s.d.n.
    lusty vigorous

  3 *perfect* instructed

  8 *buy no land* cf. the proverb 'he that buys land buys many stones' (Tilley L 52)

 11–12 *hope ... anchor* An anchor sometimes appeared in emblems depicting hope;
    see A. Henkel and A. Schöne, *Emblemata* (Stuttgart, 1967), col. 1559.

 15 *powers ... celestial* a reference to the Neo-Platonic figure of Venus Coelestis
    (Heavenly Love) who possesses the minds of honourable men whose intellects
    pass beyond the sphere of the senses towards heavenly things; see Erwin
    Panofsky, *Studies in Iconology* (Oxford, 1939), pp. 142–3

up like a flirt-gill, and sing bawdy songs upon me; but,   20
i'faith, if I live, George –

CITIZEN

Let me alone, sweetheart; I have a trick in my head shall
lodge him in the Arches for one year, and make him sing
peccavi ere I leave him, and yet he shall never know who
hurt him neither.   25

WIFE

Do, my good George, do.

[*Enter a* BOY]

CITIZEN

What shall we have Rafe do now, boy?

BOY

You shall have what you will, sir.

CITIZEN

Why, so, sir; go and fetch me him then, and let the Sophy
of Persia come and christen him a child.   30

BOY

Believe me, sir, that will not do so well. 'Tis stale; it has
been had before at the Red Bull.

WIFE

George, let Rafe travel over great hills, and let him be very
weary, and come to the King of Cracovia's house, covered
with velvet, and there let the king's daughter stand in her   35
window all in beaten gold, combing her golden locks with
a comb of ivory, and let her spy Rafe, and fall in love with

---

20 *flirt-gill* wanton

23 *Arches* The Ecclesiastical Court of Appeal for the Province of Canterbury that
sat in the Church of St Mary de Arcubus in Cheapside. 'It took cognisance of all
matters coming under ecclesiastical Law, such as marriage and divorce, wills,
abuses in the Church etc.' (Sugden). The Citizen implies that there was a prison
attached to the Court.

23–4 *sing peccavi* pay a heavy penance ('*peccavi*', Latin 'I have sinned')

29–30 *Sophy ... child* The Sophy of Persia stands godfather to Robert Sherley's
child in the last scene of Day, Rowley, and Wilkins's *The Travels of the Three
English Brothers* (1607) which had been acted at the Red Bull, the popular
theatre in Clerkenwell, built about 1605. The boy sneers because spectacular
plays that would not please the elite (*The Travels* is a good example) were presented there; *the Sophy of Persia* the Shah of Persia.

34 *Cracovia* Krakow, the capital of Poland from 1320–1609

34–7 *covered ... ivory* The Revels accounts for the romantic plays presented at
court reveal how extravagant some of the productions were. Such a 'house'
would have been a three dimensional structure standing on the stage (Hattaway,
pp. 37–9).

him, and come down to him, and carry him into her
father's house, and then let Rafe talk with her.

CITIZEN

Well said, Nell, it shall be so. – Boy, let's ha't done quickly.   40

BOY

Sir, if you will imagine all this to be done already, you shall
hear them talk, together. But we cannot present a house
covered with black velvet, and a lady in beaten gold.

CITIZEN

Sir boy, let's ha't as you can, then.

BOY

Besides, it will show ill-favouredly to have a grocer's   45
prentice to court a king's daughter.

CITIZEN

Will it so, sir? You are well read in histories! I pray you,
what was Sir Dagonet? Was not he prentice to a grocer in
London? Read the play of *The Four Prentices of London*,
where they toss their pikes so. I pray you, fetch him in, sir,   50
fetch him in.

BOY

It shall be done. – It is not our fault, gentlemen.   *Exit*

WIFE

Now we shall see fine doings, I warrant'ee, George.

> *Enter* RAFE *and the* LADY [POMPIONA], [TIM *as*] *Squire
> and* [GEORGE *as*] *Dwarf*

Oh, here they come; how prettily the King of Cracovia's
daughter is dressed.   55

CITIZEN

Ay, Nell, it is the fashion of that country, I warrant'ee.

LADY

Welcome, sir knight, unto my father's court,

---

43 *beaten gold* gold foil

45 *show ill-favouredly* seem unfitting

48 *Sir Dagonet* He was in fact King Arthur's fool; cf. Malory's *Morte d'Arthur*, ix.
19. The Citizen probably knew Sir Dagonet from Arthur's Show, an exhibition
of archery at Mile End by London citizens who assumed the arms and names of
knights of the Round Table; see 2 *Henry IV*, III.ii.73.

49 *The Four Prentices of London* In Heywood's play Eustace and Guy 'before
entering upon a combat with each other, toss and catch their pikes to prove their
strength of arm' (Murch).

53 s.d. ed. (after 55 Q1)

King of Moldavia; unto me, Pompiona,
His daughter dear. But sure you do not like
Your entertainment, that will stay with us   60
No longer but a night.
RAFE   Damsel right fair,
I am on many sad adventures bound,
That call me forth into the wilderness;
Besides, my horse's back is something galled,
Which will enforce me ride a sober pace.   65
But many thanks, fair Lady, be to you,
For using errant knight with courtesy.
LADY
But say, brave knight, what is your name and birth?
RAFE
My name is Rafe; I am an Englishman,
As true as steel, a hearty Englishman,   70
And prentice to a grocer in the Strand
By deed indent, of which I have one part.
But Fortune calling me to follow arms,
On me this holy order I did take
Of Burning Pestle, which in all men's eyes   75
I bear, confounding ladies' enemies.
LADY
Oft have I heard of your brave countrymen,
And fertile soil and store of wholesome food;
My father oft will tell me of a drink
In England found, and 'nipitato' called,   80
Which driveth all the sorrow from your hearts.
RAFE
Lady, 'tis true, you need not lay your lips
To better nipitato than there is.
LADY
And of a wild fowl he will often speak

58 *Moldavia* One of the Danubian provinces, part of which lies in modern Romania, the remainder in Moldavia. From 1601–18 Moldavia recognised Polish suzerainty (see 34). The Prince of Moldova was with the Turkish Ambassador at the English Court in November 1607.
60 *entertainment, that* reception, you who
64 *galled* sore from chafing
71 *Strand* Q2 (strond Q1); running from Fleet Street to Charing Cross, it was at this time lined with fashionable houses
72 *deed indent* Articles of agreement between master and prentice were drawn up in duplicate on one document which was then divided along an irregular line. The two parts could be proved genuine if their edges matched exactly.
80 *nipitato* prime ale

Which 'powdered beef and mustard' callèd is.   85
For there have been great wars 'twixt us and you;
But truly, Rafe, it was not long of me.
Tell me then, Rafe, could you contented be
To wear a lady's favour in your shield?

RAFE
I am a knight of religious order,   90
And will not wear a favour of a lady's
That trusts in Antichrist and false traditions.

CITIZEN
Well said, Rafe, convert her if thou canst. *a true problem-solve*

RAFE
Besides, I have a lady of my own
In merry England, for whose virtuous sake   95
I took these arms, and Susan is her name,
A cobbler's maid in Milk Street, whom I vow
Ne'er to forsake whilst life and pestle last.

LADY
Happy that cobbling dame, whoe'er she be,
That for her own, dear Rafe, hath gotten thee;   100
Unhappy I, that ne'er shall see the day
To see thee more, that bear'st my heart away.

RAFE
Lady, farewell; I needs must take my leave.

LADY
Hard-hearted Rafe, that ladies dost deceive.

CITIZEN
Hark thee, Rafe, there's money for thee; give something in   105
the King of Cracovia's house; be not beholding to him.

RAFE
Lady, before I go, I must remember
Your father's officers, who, truth to tell,
Have been about me very diligent.
Hold up thy snowy hand, thou princely maid: 110
There's twelve pence for your father's chamberlain;
And another shilling for his cook
For, by my troth, the goose was roasted well;

---

85 *powdered* salted
87 *long of* on account of
89 *favour* token of affection such as a glove or scarf
99 *cobbling* pun on cobble = bungle

And twelve pence for your father's horse-keeper,
For 'nointing my horse' back; and for his butter,   115
There is another shilling; to the maid
That washed my boot-hose, there's an English groat;
And twopence to the boy that wiped my boots;
And last, fair lady, there is for yourself
Threepence, to buy you pins at Bumbo Fair.   120

LADY
Full many thanks; and I will keep them safe
Till all the heads be off, for thy sake, Rafe.

RAFE
Advance, my squire and dwarf; I cannot stay.

LADY
Thou kill'st my heart in parting thus away.

Exeunt

WIFE
I commend Rafe yet that he will not stoop to a Cracovian.   125
There's properer women in London than any are there,
iwis.

Enter MERCHANT, HUMPHREY, LUCE, *and a* BOY
[LUCE *kneels*]

But here comes Master Humphrey and his love again now,
George.

CITIZEN
Ay, cony, peace.   130

MERCHANT
Go, get you up; I will not be entreated.
And, gossip mine, I'll keep you sure hereafter

---

115 *butter* perhaps in order to grease the hay of horses so that they would not eat so
    much – a trick of dishonest ostlers
117 *boot-hose* stockings covering the upper part of the leg often elaborately embroi-
    dered
118 *boots* worn by gallants and would-be gentlemen
120 *pins* Elaborate pins were fashionable.
    Bumbo The word probably comes from the name of a drink made from rum,
    water, and nutmeg, doubtless drunk at fairs.
125 *stoop* submit
126 *properer* handsomer
127 s.d. ed. (after 130 Q1)
131 *up* either from her knees or to her chamber
132 *gossip* gadabout

From gadding out again with boys and unthrifts.
Come, they are women's tears; I know your fashion. –
Go, sirrah, lock her in, and keep the key   135
Safe as you love your life.

Exeunt LUCE *and* BOY

                    Now, my son Humphrey,
You may both rest assurèd of my love
In this, and reap your own desire.
HUMPHREY
I see this love you speak of, through your daughter,
Although the hole be little; and hereafter   140
Will yield the like in all I may, or can,
Fitting a Christian, and a gentleman.
MERCHANT
I do believe you, my good son, and thank you:
For 'twere an impudence to think you flattered.
HUMPHREY
It were indeed; but shall I tell you why?   145
I have been beaten twice about the lie.
MERCHANT
Well, son, no more of compliment. My daughter
Is yours again; appoint the time, and take her;
We'll have no stealing for it. I myself
And some few of our friends will see you married.   150
HUMPHREY
I would you would, i'faith, for, be it known,
I ever was afraid to lie alone.
MERCHANT
Some three days hence, then.
HUMPHREY   Three days? Let me see:
'Tis somewhat of the most; yet I agree
Because I mean against the appointed day   155
To visit all my friends in new array.

Enter SERVANT

SERVANT
Sir, there's a gentlewoman without would speak with your
worship.

133 *unthrifts* prodigals
136 s.d. *Exeunt* ed. (*Exit* Q1)
139–42 Humphrey's extended conceit is preposterous and (unintentionally?) obscene
139 *daughter* to rhyme with hereafter
149 *We'll . . . it.* There will not be another elopement.
154 *of . . . most* over-long
155 *against* in expectation of

MERCHANT
 What is she?
SERVANT
 Sir, I asked her not.   160
MERCHANT
 Bid her come in.

                                        [*Exit* SERVANT]

             Enter MISTRESS MERRYTHOUGHT *and* MICHAEL

MISTRESS MERRYTHOUGHT
 Peace be to your worship. I come as a poor suitor to you,
 sir, in the behalf of this child.
MERCHANT
 Are you not wife to Merrythought?
MISTRESS MERRYTHOUGHT
 Yes, truly; would I had ne'er seen his eyes! He has undone   165
 me and himself and his children, and there he lives at home,
 and sings and hoits and revels among his drunken
 companions; but, I warrant you, where to get a penny to
 put bread in his mouth he knows not and therefore, if it like
 your worship, I would entreat your letter to the honest host   170
 of the Bell in Waltham, that I may place my child under the
 protection of his tapster, in some settled course of life.
MERCHANT
 I'm glad the heavens have heard my prayers. Thy husband,
 When I was ripe in sorrows, laughed at me;
 Thy son, like an unthankful wretch, I having   175
 Redeemed him from his fall and made him mine,
 To show his love again, first stole my daughter,
 Then wronged this gentleman, and, last of all,
 Gave me that grief had almost brought me down
 Unto my grave, had not a stronger hand   180
 Relieved my sorrows. Go, and weep as I did,
 And be unpitied; for I here profess
 An everlasting hate to all thy name.
MISTRESS MERRYTHOUGHT
 Will you so, sir? How say you by that? – Come, Mick, let
 him keep his wind to cool his porridge. We'll go to thy   185

---

165 *He* Q3 (ha Q1)
167 *hoits* indulges in riotous mirth
179 *grief* sorrow which (Abbott, 399)
185 *keep ... porridge* (Tilley W422)

nurse's, Mick; she knits silk stockings, boy, and we'll knit
too, boy, and be beholding to none of them all.

Exeunt MICHAEL *and Mother* [MISTRESS MERRYTHOUGHT]

Enter a BOY *with a letter*

BOY
  Sir, I take it you are the master of this house.
MERCHANT
  How then, boy?
BOY
  Then to yourself, sir, comes this letter.   190
MERCHANT
  From whom, my pretty boy?
BOY
  From him that was your servant; but no more
  Shall that name ever be, for he is dead:
  Grief of your purchased anger broke his heart.
  I saw him die, and from his hand received   195
  This paper, with a charge to bring it hither;
  Read it, and satisfy yourself in all.

Letter

MERCHANT [*reads*]
  'Sir, that I have wronged your love, I must confess; in which
  I have purchased to myself, besides mine own undoing, the
  ill opinion of my friends. Let not your anger, good sir, out- 200
  live me, but suffer me to rest in peace with your forgiveness;
  let my body (if a dying man may so much prevail with you)
  be brought to your daughter, that she may truly know my
  hot flames are now buried, and, withal, receive a testimony
  of the zeal I bore her virtue. Farewell for ever, and be ever 205
  happy, Jasper.'
  God's hand is great in this. I do forgive him;
  Yet I am glad he's quiet, where I hope
  He will not bite again. – Boy, bring the body,
  And let him have his will, if that be all.   210
BOY
  'Tis here without, sir.
MERCHANT   So, sir, if you please,
  You may conduct it in; I do not fear it.
HUMPHREY
  I'll be your usher, boy, for though I say it,
  He owed me something once, and well did pay it.

194 *purchased* incurred by his conduct

Exeunt

Enter LUCE *alone*

LUCE
If there be any punishment inflicted   215
Upon the miserable, more than yet I feel,
Let it together seize me, and at once
Press down my soul. I cannot bear the pain
Of these delaying tortures. Thou that art
The end of all, and the sweet rest of all,   220
Come, come, oh Death, bring me to thy peace,
And blot out all the memory I nourish
Both of my father and my cruel friend.
Oh wretched maid, still living to be wretched,
To be a say to Fortune in her changes,   225
And grow to number times and woes together!
How happy had I been, if, being born,
My grave had been my cradle.

Enter SERVANT

SERVANT   By your leave,
Young mistress, here's a boy hath brought a coffin.
What 'a would say, I know not, but your father   230
Charged me to give you notice. Here they come.   [*Exit*]

Enter two [a CARRIER *and a* BOY] *bearing a coffin,*
JASPER *in it*

LUCE
For me I hope 'tis come, and 'tis most welcome.
BOY
Fair mistress, let me not add greater grief
To that great store you have already. Jasper,
That whilst he lived was yours, now dead   235
And here enclosed, commanded me to bring
His body hither, and to crave a tear
From those fair eyes, though he deserved not pity,
To deck his funeral; for so he bid me
Tell her for whom he died.

217 *together* altogether
225 *say* <assay, object for testing
231 s.d. *two* More carriers are probably required – see IV, 2.
232 *hope* Q2 (hop't Q1)

LUCE   He shall have many.   240
  – Good friends, depart a little, whilst I take
  My leave of this dead man that once I loved:

Exeunt COFFIN CARRIER *and* BOY

  Hold yet a little, life, and then I give thee
  To thy first heavenly being. Oh, my friend!
  Hast thou deceived me thus, and got before me?   245
  I shall not long be after. But, believe me,
  Thou wert too cruel, Jasper, 'gainst thyself
  In punishing the fault I could have pardoned,
  With so untimely death. Thou didst not wrong me,
  But ever wert most kind, most true, most loving;   250
  And I the most unkind, most false, most cruel.
  Didst thou but ask a tear I'll give thee all,
  Even all my eyes can pour down, all my sighs,
  And all myself, before thou goest from me.
  These are but sparing rites; but if thy soul   255
  Be yet about this place, and can behold
  And see what I prepare to deck thee with,
  It shall go up, borne on the wings of peace,
  And satisfied. First will I sing thy dirge,
  Then kiss thy pale lips, and then die myself,   260
  And fill one coffin and one grave together.

Song

    Come you whose loves are dead,
      And whilst I sing
      Weep and wring
    Every hand and every head,   265
    Bind with cypress and sad yew,
    Ribands black, and candles blue,
    For him that was of men most true.

    Come with heavy moaning,
      And on his grave   270
      Let him have
    Sacrifice of sighs and groaning,

---

255 *These* ed. (There Q1)
    sparing restrained
266 *cypress . . . yew* also used as emblems of mourning in 'Come away, come away,
    death' in *Twelfth Night*, II.iv.50 ff.
267 *blue* the colour of constancy
269 *moaning* ed. (mourning Q1)

> Let him have fair flowers enow,
> White and purple, green and yellow,
> For him that was of men most true.   275

Thou sable cloth, sad cover of my joys,
I lift thee up, and thus I meet with death.

JASPER [*rising out of the coffin*]
  And thus you meet the living.
LUCE   Save me, heaven!
JASPER
  Nay, do not fly me, fair; I am no spirit;
  Look better on me; do you know me yet?   280
LUCE
  Oh, thou dear shadow of my friend.
JASPER   Dear substance;
  I swear I am no shadow; feel my hand,
  It is the same it was. I am your Jasper,
  Your Jasper that's yet living, and yet loving.
  Pardon my rash attempt, my foolish proof   285
  I put in practice of your constancy;
  For sooner should my sword have drunk my blood
  And set my soul at liberty than drawn
  The least drop from that body; for which boldness
  Doom me to anything: if death, I take it,   290
  And willingly.
LUCE   This death I'll give you for it.

                                      [*Kisses him*]

  So, now I am satisfied; you are no spirit,
  But my own truest, truest, truest friend.
  Why do you come thus to me?
JASPER   First to see you,
  Then to convey you hence.
LUCE   It cannot be,   295
  For I am locked up here and watched at all hours,
  That 'tis impossible for me to 'scape.
JASPER
  Nothing more possible. Within this coffin
  Do you convey yourself; let me alone,
  I have the wits of twenty men about me.   300

---

277 s.d. There is a similar moment in Middleton's *The Family of Love* (1603), II.iv.
281 *shadow* shade, departed spirit
290 *death* playing with the erotic connotations of 'death' (orgasm)
293 *friend.* ed. (friend, Q1)

Only I crave the shelter of your closet
A little, and then fear me not. Creep in,
That they may presently convey you hence.
Fear nothing, dearest love; I'll be your second.

> [LUCE *lies down in the coffin, and* JASPER *covers her*
> *with the cloth*]

Lie close, so; all goes well yet. – Boy!   305

> [*Enter* BOY *and* COFFIN CARRIER]

BOY
At hand, sir.
JASPER
Convey away the coffin, and be wary.
BOY
'Tis done already.
JASPER
Now must I go conjure.   *Exit*

> *Enter* MERCHANT

MERCHANT
Boy, boy!   310
BOY
Your servant, sir.
MERCHANT
Do me this kindness, boy (hold, here's a crown): before
thou bury the body of this fellow, carry it to his old merry
father, and salute him from me, and bid him sing; he hath
cause.   315
BOY
I will, sir.
MERCHANT
And then bring me word what tune he is in, and have
another crown; but do it truly. I have fitted him a bargain
now will vex him.
BOY
God bless your worship's health, sir. *feels sarcastic*   320

301 *closet* private chamber
302 *fear me not* do not fear for me
304 *second* support
305 *close* hidden
309 *conjure* arrange my deceptions
317 *tune* mood
318 *fitted* furnished with

MERCHANT
  Farewell, boy.

                                              Exeunt

              Enter MASTER MERRYTHOUGHT

WIFE
  Ah, old Merrythought, art thou there again? Let's hear
  some of thy songs.

OLD MERRYTHOUGHT [SINGS]
    Who can sing a merrier note
    Than he that cannot change a groat?   325
  Not a denier left, and yet my heart leaps. I do wonder yet,
  as old as I am, that any man will follow a trade, or serve,
  that may sing and laugh, and walk the streets. My wife and
  both my sons are I know not where; I have nothing left, nor
  know I how to come by meat to supper; yet am I merry still, 330
  for I know I shall find it upon the table at six o'clock. oh You poor
  Therefore, hang thought. [*sings*]   fool
    I would not be a serving man
    To carry the cloak-bag still,
    Nor would I be a falconer   335
    The greedy hawks to fill;
    But I would be in a good house,
    And have a good master too,
    But I would eat and drink of the best,
    And no work would I do.   340
  This is it that keeps life and soul together: mirth. This is the
  philosophers' stone that they write so much on, that keeps
  a man ever young.

                Enter a BOY

BOY
  Sir, they say they know all your money is gone, and they
  will trust you for no more drink.   345

324–5 *Who ... groat* This catch is given in Ravenscroft's *Pammelia* (1601), ed.
    Warlock (Oxford, 1928), p. 26; it was proverbial (Tilley N249).
325 *groat* a coin worth four pence
326 *denier* French coin, a twelfth of a sou, hence a very small sum
333–40 (song printed on four lines Q1–3, F)
334 *cloak-bag* portmanteau
342 *philosophers' stone* the reputed alchemical substance that could transmute base
    metal into gold and offer healing properties and everlasting life

OLD MERRYTHOUGHT

Will they not? Let 'em choose. The best is, I have mirth at
home, and need not send abroad for that; let them keep
their drink to themselves. [*sings*]
> For Jillian of Bury she dwells on a hill,
> And she hath good beer and ale to sell,   350
> And of good fellows she thinks no ill;
>> And thither will we go now, now, now, now,
>> And thither will we go now.

> And when you have made a little stay,
> You need not ask what is to pay,   355
> But kiss your hostess and go your way;
>> And thither, etc.

Enter another BOY

2 BOY

Sir, I can get no bread for supper.

OLD MERRYTHOUGHT

Hang bread and supper! Let's preserve our mirth, and we
shall never feel hunger, I'll warrant you. Let's have a catch;   360
boy, follow me; come, sing this catch:
[*They sing*]
> Ho, ho, nobody at home!
> Meat, nor drink, nor money ha' we none.
> Fill the pot, Eedy,
> Never more need I.   365

So, boys, enough; follow me; let's change our place and we
shall laugh afresh.

Exeunt

Finis Act 4

360 *catch* song sung as a round
361 *sing this catch* these words are separated from the preceding 'come' by a space
      of 12.5 mm. in Q1–2 and may have been intended as a stage direction
362–5 (printed as prose in Q1–3, F)
      Ho, ho, nobody at home? Another catch from *Pammelia*, 85, ed. Warlock, p. 12.
367 *Finis Act 4* Q1–3, F print below line 62 of following interlude

[Interlude IV]

WIFE

Let him go, George; 'a shall not have any countenance from us, nor a good word from any i'th' company, if I may strike stroke in't.

CITIZEN

No more 'a sha'not, love; but, Nell, I will have Rafe do a very notable matter now, to the eternal honour and glory 5
of all grocers. – Sirrah, you there, boy! Can none of you hear?

[*Enter* BOY]

BOY

Sir, your pleasure.

CITIZEN

Let Rafe come out on May Day in the morning, and speak upon a conduit with all his scarfs about him, and his 10
feathers and his rings and his knacks.

BOY

Why, sir, you do not think of our plot. What will become of that, then?

CITIZEN

Why, sir, I care not what become on't. I'll have him come out, or I'll fetch him out myself. I'll have something done in 15
honour of the city. Besides, he hath been long enough upon adventures. Bring him out quickly, or, if I come in amongst you –

BOY

Well, sir, he shall come out. But if our play miscarry, sir, you are like to pay for't. *Exit* BOY 20

CITIZEN

Bring him away, then.

WIFE

This will be brave, i'faith; George, shall not he dance the morris too for the credit of the Strand?

---

1 *countenance* favour

2–3 *strike stroke* have my say

9 *May Day* For the classic account of May Day festivities see Stubbes, Ch. xiii.

10 *conduit* cistern, fountain

10–11 *scarfs ... knacks* the accoutrements of Morris dancers; for the dance, see Laroque, pp. 119–36

11 *knacks* trinkets

CITIZEN

No, sweetheart, it will be too much for the boy.

Enter RAFE

Oh, there he is, Nell; he's reasonable well in reparel, but he has not rings enough.

RAFE

London, to thee I do present the merry month of May;
Let each true subject be content to hear me what I say:
For from the top of conduit head, as plainly may appear,
I will both tell my name to you and wherefore I came
   here.
My name is Rafe, by due descent though not ignoble I,
Yet far inferior to the flock of gracious grocery;
And by the Common Council of my fellows in the Strand,
With gilded staff and crossèd scarf, the May-lord here I
   stand.
Rejoice, oh English hearts, rejoice; rejoice, oh lovers dear;
Rejoice, oh city, town, and country; rejoice eke every
   shire.
For now the fragrant flowers do spring and sprout in
   seemly sort,
The little birds do sit and sing, the lambs do make fine
   sport.
And now the birchen tree doth bud, that makes the
   school-boy cry;
The morris rings while hobby-horse doth foot it
   feateously.
The lords and ladies now abroad for their disport and
   play,
Do kiss sometimes upon the grass, and sometimes in the
   hay.

Now butter with a leaf of sage is good to purge the blood;
Fly Venus and phlebotomy, for they are neither good.
Now little fish on tender stone begin to cast their bellies,　　45
And sluggish snails, that erst were mute, do creep out of
　their shellies.
The rumbling rivers now do warm for little boys to
　paddle,
The sturdy steed now goes to grass, and up they hang his
　saddle.
The heavy hart, the bellowing buck, the rascal, and the
　pricket,
Are now among the yeoman's peas, and leave the fearful
　thicket.　　50
And be like them, oh you, I say, of this same noble town,
And lift aloft your velvet heads, and, slipping off your
　gown,
With bells on legs and napkins clean unto your shoulders
　tied,
With scarfs and garters as you please, and 'Hey for our
　town' cried,
March out, and show your willing minds, by twenty and
　by twenty,　　55
To Hogsdon or to Newington, where ale and cakes are
　plenty.
And let it ne'er be said for shame, that we the youths of
　London
Lay thrumming of our caps at home, and left our custom
　undone.

---

43 *butter* supposed to have medicinal properties in May
44 *Venus* Intercourse was thought to entail, like blood-letting (phlebotomy), a loss
　of 'spirit'.
45 *cast ... bellies* spawn
46 *snails* 'Snails were used in love divinations: they were set to crawl on the hearth,
　and were thought to mark in the ashes the initials of the lover's name' (Brand,
　ii. 553). There is no need to emend 'mute' (unrevealing) to 'mewed' = 'confined'.
　erst formerly
49 *rascal* young or inferior deer of herd
　pricket buck in its second year
52 *velvet heads* 'A sly allusion to the horns of the citizens' (Dyce). The new antlers
　of a deer are velvety.
53–4 *bells ... garters* the accoutrements of the Morris
56 *Hogsdon ... Newington* the one a district north of London, the other a suburb
　south of Southwark; both were favourite places for afternoon excursions
58 *thrumming ... caps* decorating our caps with tassels = wasting time
　custom wenching

Up then, I say, both young and old, both man and maid
   a-maying,
With drums and guns that bounce aloud, and merry tabor
   playing,   60
Which to prolong, God save our king, and send his
   country peace,
And root out treason from the land! And so, my friends, I
   cease.   *[Exit]*

Act V

Enter MERCHANT, *solus*

MERCHANT
I will have no great store of company at the wedding: a
couple of neighbours and their wives; and we will have a
capon in stewed broth, with marrow, and a good piece of
beef, stuck with rosemary.

Enter JASPER, *his face mealed*

JASPER
Forbear thy pains, fond man; it is too late.   5
MERCHANT
Heaven bless me! Jasper?
JASPER   Ay, I am his ghost,
Whom thou hast injured for his constant love,
Fond worldly wretch, who dost not understand
In death that true hearts cannot parted be.
First, know thy daughter is quite borne away   10
On wings of angels, through the liquid air,
To far out of thy reach, and never more
Shalt thou behold her face. But she and I
Will in another world enjoy our loves,
Where neither father's anger, poverty,   15
Nor any cross that troubles earthly men

---

60 *tabor* small drum
62 *treason* a possible allusion to the Gunpowder Plot of 1605

Act V ed. (Actus 5. Scoena prima Q1)
  4 *rosemary* often used at weddings
  4 s.d. *mealed* whitened with flour
  5 *pains* efforts
 11 *liquid* clear, transparent
 16 *cross* impediment

Shall make us sever our united hearts.
And never shalt thou sit, or be alone
In any place, but I will visit thee
With ghastly looks, and put into thy mind   20
The great offences which thou didst to me.
When thou art at thy table with thy friends,
Merry in heart, and filled with swelling wine,
I'll come in midst of all thy pride and mirth,
Invisible to all men but thyself,   25
And whisper such a sad tale in thine ear
Shall make thee let the cup fall from thy hand,
And stand as mute and pale as Death itself.

MERCHANT
Forgive me, Jasper. Oh, what might I do,
Tell me, to satisfy thy troubled ghost?   30

JASPER
There is no means; too late thou think'st of this.

MERCHANT
But tell me what were best for me to do.

JASPER
Repent thy deed, and satisfy my father,
And beat fond Humphrey out of thy doors!   *Exit* JASPER

Enter HUMPHREY

WIFE
Look, George, his very ghost would have folks beaten.   35

HUMPHREY   Poor
Father, my bride is gone, fair Mistress Luce;
My soul's the fount of vengeance, mischief's sluice. Humphrey

MERCHANT
Hence, fool, out of my sight with thy fond passion!
Thou hast undone me.

[*Beats him*]

HUMPHREY   Hold, my father dear,
For Luce thy daughter's sake, that had no peer.   40

MERCHANT
Thy father, fool? There's some blows more, begone!
Jasper, I hope thy ghost be well appeased

18ff. The passage recalls the visit of Banquo's Ghost to Macbeth (III.iv).

33 *satisfy* compensate

37 *sluice* conduit

38 *passion*! ed. (passion Q1) *passion* = grief

To see thy will performed. Now will I go
To satisfy thy father for thy wrongs.   *Exit*

HUMPHREY

What shall I do? I have been beaten twice,   45
And Mistress Luce is gone. Help me, device!
Since my true love is gone, I nevermore,
Whilst I do live, upon the sky will pore;
But in the dark will wear out my shoe soles
In passion in Saint Faith's Church under Paul's.   *Exit*   50

WIFE

George, call Rafe hither; if you love me, call Rafe hither. I
have the bravest thing for him to do, George; prithee call
him quickly.

CITIZEN

Rafe, why Rafe, boy!

Enter RAFE

RAFE

Here, sir.   55

CITIZEN

Come hither, Rafe; come to thy mistress, boy.

WIFE

Rafe, I would have thee call all the youths together in
battle-ray, with drums, and guns, and flags, and march to
Mile End in pompous fashion, and there exhort your
soldiers to be merry and wise, and to keep their beards   60
from burning, Rafe; and then skirmish, and let your flags
fly, and cry, 'Kill, kill, kill'! My husband shall lend you his
jerkin, Rafe, and there's a scarf; for the rest, the house shall
furnish you, and we'll pay for't. Do it bravely, Rafe, and
think before whom you perform, and what person you   65
represent.

---

46 *device* contrivance
50 *Faith's Church* 'At the West end of this Jesus Chapel, under the choir of Paul's,
    also was a parish Church of Saint Faith, commonly called St Faith under Paul's'
    (Stow, i. 329). Gallants used to promenade in the aisle of the cathedral above, so
    Humphrey has chosen a fitting retreat.
52 *bravest* most splendid
58 *battle-ray* battle order
59 *pompous* ceremonial
60–61 *keep ... burning* prevent the accidental discharge of the matchlocks of their
    muskets
63 *house* theatre

RAFE

I warrant you, mistress, if I do it not for the honour of the
city and the credit of my master, let me never hope for
freedom.

WIFE

'Tis well spoken, i'faith. Go thy ways; thou art a spark   70
indeed.

CITIZEN

Rafe, Rafe, double your files bravely, Rafe.

RAFE

I warrant you, sir.   *Exit* RAFE

CITIZEN

Let him look narrowly to his service; I shall take him else.
I was there myself a pikeman once in the hottest of the day,   75
wench; had my feather shot sheer away, the fringe of my
pike burnt off with powder, my pate broken with a
scouring-stick, and yet I thank God I am here.

Drum within

WIFE

Hark, George, the drums.

CITIZEN

Ran, tan, tan, tan; ran, tan. Oh, wench, an thou hadst but   80
seen little Ned of Aldgate, Drum-Ned, how he made it roar
again, and laid on like a tyrant, and then struck softly till
the ward came up, and then thundered again, and together
we go. 'Sa, sa, sa, bounce', quoth the guns; 'Courage, my
hearts', quoth the captains; 'Saint George', quoth the   85
pikemen; and withal here they lay, and there they lay. And
yet for all this I am here, wench.

69 *freedom* rank of freeman in the Grocers' Guild
70 *spark* smart young man
72 *double ... files* combine your two ranks in an elaborate manoeuvre; see S. Lee
    and C. T. Onions, (ed.), *Shakespeare's England*, 2 vols. (Oxford, 1916), i. 114
74 *narrowly* closely
    service manoeuvres
    take reprehend
78 *scouring-stick* for cleaning out a gun
81 *Aldgate* a ward in the east of the City
82 *tyrant* a stock character in the mystery plays (Herod is an example)
83 *ward* detachment of militia
84 *Sa, sa, sa* 'an imitation of the sputter and hiss of the slow-burning match'
    (Zitner)
    bounce thump, bang

WIFE

Be thankful for it, George, for indeed 'tis wonderful.

Enter RAFE *and his company, with drums and colours*

RAFE

March fair, my hearts! Lieutenant, beat the rear up. – Ancient, let your colours fly; but have a great care of the 90 butchers' hooks at Whitechapel; they have been the death of many a fair ancient. – Open your files that I may take a view both of your persons and munition. – Sergeant, call a muster.

SERGEANT

A stand! – William Hamerton, pewterer!   95

HAMERTON

Here, captain.

RAFE

A corslet and a Spanish pike; 'tis well. Can you shake it with a terror?

HAMERTON

I hope so, captain.

RAFE

Charge upon me.   100

[HAMERTON *charges upon* RAFE]

'Tis with the weakest. Put more strength, William Hamerton, more strength. As you were again. – Proceed, Sergeant.

SERGEANT

George Greengoose, poulterer!

GREENGOOSE

Here.   105

RAFE

Let me see your piece, neighbour Greengoose; when was she shot in?

89 *beat ... up* round up, stir up with a drum-roll
90 *Ancient* Ensign-bearer
91 *Whitechapel* a parish east of Aldgate; there was a row of butchers' shops along one side of the Whitechapel Road
94 *muster* roll
95 *A stand* 'Attention'
97 *corslet* armour covering the body
106 *piece* firearm; the whole of this scene contains bawdy puns

GREENGOOSE

An't like you, master captain, I made a shot even now,
partly to scour her, and partly for audacity.

RAFE

It should seem so certainly, for her breath is yet inflamed; 110
besides, there is a main fault in the touch-hole, it runs and
stinketh; and I tell you moreover, and believe it, ten such
touch-holes would breed the pox in the army. Get you a
feather, neighbour, get you a feather, sweet oil, and paper,
and your piece may do well enough yet. Where's your 115
powder!

GREENGOOSE

Here.

RAFE

What, in a paper? As I am a soldier and a gentleman, it
craves a martial court. You ought to die for't. Where's your
horn? Answer me to that.   120

GREENGOOSE

An't like you, sir, I was oblivious.

RAFE

It likes me not you should be so; 'tis a shame for you, and
a scandal to all our neighbours, being a man of worth and
estimation, to leave your horn behind you: I am afraid 'twill
breed example. But let me tell you no more on't. – Stand, 125
till I view you all. – What's become o'th'nose of your flask?

1 SOLDIER

Indeed la, captain, 'twas blown away with powder.

RAFE

Put on a new one at the city's charge. – Where's the stone
of this piece?

2 SOLDIER

The drummer took it out to light tobacco.   130

RAFE

'Tis a fault, my friend; put it in again. – You want a nose –
and you a stone. – Sergeant, take a note on't, for I mean to
stop it in the pay. – Remove, and march! Soft and fair,

---

108 *An't* ed. (And Q1)
114 *feather ... paper* to clean their guns
120 *horn* powder-horn and cuckold's horn
121 *oblivious* forgetful
128 *stone* flint
131 *want a nose* alluding to the effects of syphilis
     want lack
132 *stone* testicle
133 *Soft and fair* Easy does it

gentlemen, soft and fair! Double your files! As you were!
Faces about! Now, you with the sodden face, keep in there!   135
Look to your match, sirrah, it will be in your fellow's flask
anon. So, make a crescent now; advance your pikes; stand,
and give ear! Gentlemen, countrymen, friends, and my
fellow-soldiers, I have brought you this day from the shops
of security and the counters of content, to measure out in   140
these furious fields honour by the ell, and prowess by the
pound. Let it not, oh, let it not, I say, be told hereafter the
noble issue of this city fainted, but bear yourselves in this
fair action like men, valiant men, and freemen. Fear not the
face of the enemy, nor the noise of the guns, for believe me,   145
brethren, the rude rumbling of a brewer's car is far more
terrible, of which you have a daily experience; neither let
the stink of powder offend you, since a more valiant stink
is nightly with you. To a resolved mind his home is everywhere. I speak not this to take away the hope of your   150
return; for you shall see, I do not doubt it, and that very
shortly, your loving wives again, and your sweet children,
whose care doth bear you company in baskets. Remember,
then, whose cause you have in hand, and like a sort of true-
born scavengers, scour me this famous realm of enemies. I   155
have no more to say but this: stand to your tacklings, lads,
and show to the world you can as well brandish a sword as
shake an apron. Saint George, and on, my hearts!

OMNES
    Saint George! Saint George!

                                                    Exeunt

WIFE
    'Twas well done, Rafe. I'll send thee a cold capon a-field,   160
    and a bottle of March beer; and it may be, come myself to
    see thee. Wink wonk

135 *sodden* stewed, or affected by the sweating treatment for the pox
136 *match* part of a musket's firing mechanism
    flask for gunpowder
137 *advance* raise from their trail position to the hip
138 ff. Rafe's exhortation to his soldiers contains echoes of Richard III's oration to
    his army, V.iii.313 ff.
141 *ell* a measure of 45 inches
153 *whose ... baskets* who show their care by sending you provisions
154 *sort* company
156 *tacklings* weapons (with a bawdy sense)
161 *March beer* strong beer

CITIZEN

Nell, the boy has deceived me much; I did not think it had
been in him. He has performed such a matter, wench, that
if I live, next year I'll have him captain of the galley-foist,   165
or I'll want my will.

Enter OLD MERRYTHOUGHT

OLD MERRYTHOUGHT

Yet, I thank God, I break not a wrinkle more than I had.
Not a stoup, boys? Care, live with cats, I defy thee! My
heart is as sound as an oak; and though I want drink to wet
my whistle, I can sing [*sings*]:   170
    Come no more there, boys, come no more there;
    For we shall never whilst we live, come any more there.

Enter a BOY [*and* COFFIN-CARRIERS] *with a coffin*

BOY

God save you, sir.

OLD MERRYTHOUGHT

It's a brave boy. Canst thou sing?

BOY

Yes, sir, I can sing, but 'tis not so necessary at this time.   175

OLD MERRYTHOUGHT [*sings*]
    Sing we, and chant it,
    Whilst love doth grant it.

BOY

Sir, sir, if you knew what I have brought you, you would
have little list to sing.

OLD MERRYTHOUGHT [*sings*]
        Oh, the minion round,   180
    Full long I have thee sought,
        And now I have thee found,
    And what hast thou here brought?

---

165 *galley-foist* state barge of the Lord Mayor
167 *Yet* Still
    break show
168 *stoup* a measure of liquor, two quarts
    Care ... cats cf. 'Care will kill a cat' (Tilley C84)
    Care, ed. (Care Q1)
176-7 *Sing ... it* words and music in Thomas Morley's *Ballets to Five Voices* (1595
    and 1600), ed. E. H. Fellowes (London, 1913), No. 4
180 *minion* ed. (Mimon Q1) a paramour
181 *long* Q2 (long long Q1)

BOY
  A coffin, sir, and your dead son Jasper in it.
OLD MERRYTHOUGHT
  Dead? [*sings*]   185
          Why, farewell he.
          Thou wast a bonny boy,
          And I did love thee.

                    Enter JASPER

JASPER
  Then, I pray you, sir, do so still.
OLD MERRYTHOUGHT
  Jasper's ghost? [*sings*]   190
          Thou art welcome from Stygian lake so soon;
          Declare to me what wondrous things in Pluto's court
              are done.
JASPER
  By my troth, sir, I ne'er came there; 'tis too hot for me, sir.
OLD MERRYTHOUGHT
  A merry ghost, a very merry ghost! [*sings*]
          And where is your true love? Oh, where is yours?   195
JASPER
  Marry, look you, sir.

              Heaves up the coffin [*and* LUCE *climbs out*]

OLD MERRYTHOUGHT
  Ah, ha! Art thou good at that, i'faith? [*sings*]
          With hey, trixy, terlery-whiskin,
          The world it runs on wheels,
          When the young man's —   200
          Up goes the maiden's heels.

          MISTRESS MERRYTHOUGHT *and* MICHAEL *within*

MISTRESS MERRYTHOUGHT [*within*]
  What, Master Merrythought, will you not let's in? What do
  you think shall become of us?
OLD MERRYTHOUGHT
  What voice is that that calleth at our door?
MISTRESS MERRYTHOUGHT [*within*]
  You know me well enough; I am sure I have not been such   205
  a stranger to you.

---

191 *Stygian lake* the river Styx at the edge of the underworld; 'lake' could mean
     'stream'
199 *world ... wheels* (Tilley W893)
200 The missing obscenity may include the word 'friskin', a wanton action.

OLD MERRYTHOUGHT [*sings*]
> And some they whistled, and some they sung,
>> Hey, down, down!
> And some did loudly say,
> Ever as the Lord Barnet's horn blew,   210
>> Away, Musgrave, away.

MISTRESS MERRYTHOUGHT [*within*]
You will not have us starve here, will you, Master Merrythought?

JASPER
Nay, good sir, be persuaded, she is my mother. If her
offences have been great against you, let your own love   215
remember she is yours, and so forgive her.

LUCE
Good Master Merrythought, let me entreat you; I will not
be denied.

MISTRESS MERRYTHOUGHT [*within*]
Why, Master Merrythought, will you be a vexed thing still?

OLD MERRYTHOUGHT
Woman, I take you to my love again; but you shall sing   220
before you enter; therefore dispatch your song and so come
in.

MISTRESS MERRYTHOUGHT [*within*]
Well, you must have your will when all's done. – Mick,
what song canst thou sing, boy?

MICHAEL
I can sing none, forsooth, but 'A Lady's Daughter of Paris'   225
properly.

207–11 *And ... away* from the ballad of 'Little Musgrave and Lady Barnard'; Child
No. 81A, music in Bronson, ii. 267 ff.

215 *own love* 'self-love' (Zitner)

219 *vexed* cantankerous

225–6 *I ... properly* from 'O man in Desperation', a broadside ballad that begins:
> It was a lady's daughter,
>> Of Paris properly,
> Her mother her commanded
>> To mass that she should hie:
> 'O pardon me, dear mother',
>> Her daughter dear did say,
> 'Unto that filthy idol
>> I never can obey'.

It is printed in *The Roxburghe Ballads* (ed. 1896), Vol. I, part I, pp. 35–7; music
in Simpson, pp. 533–6.

226 *properly* Michael plays on the fact that this word occurs in the song itself.

MISTRESS MERRYTHOUGHT [*and* MICHAEL *within*]

Song

It was a lady's daughter, etc.

[OLD MERRYTHOUGHT *admits* MISTRESS MERRYTHOUGHT
and MICHAEL]

OLD MERRYTHOUGHT
Come, you're welcome home again. [*sings*]
  If such danger be in playing,
  And jest must to earnest turn,   230
  You shall go no more a-maying.
MERCHANT [*within*]
Are you within, sir? Master Merrythought.
JASPER
It is my master's voice. Good sir, go hold him in talk, whilst
we convey ourselves into some inward room.

          [*Exit with* LUCE]

OLD MERRYTHOUGHT
What are you? Are you merry? You must be very merry if 235
you enter.
MERCHANT [*within*]
I am, sir.
OLD MERRYTHOUGHT
Sing then.
MERCHANT [*within*]
Nay, good sir, open to me.
OLD MERRYTHOUGHT
Sing, I say, or, by the merry heart, you come not in. 240
MERCHANT [*within*]
Well, sir, I'll sing: [*sings*]
  Fortune my foe, etc.

229–31 *If ... a-maying* The refrain of Thomas Campion's song 'My Love hath
 vowed' included in Philip Rosseter's *Book of Ayres* (1601), No. 5; text in Walter
 R. Davies, (ed.), *The Works of Thomas Campion*, (London, 1969), p. 27, music
 in Thurston Dart, ed. *The English Lute Songs*, Series I, iv, xiii, pp. 8–9.
229 *playing* copulation
242 *Fortune my foe* One of the most popular songs of the period; the first stanza is:
    Fortune my foe, why dost thou frown on me?
    And will thy favours never better be?
    Wilt thou, I say, for ever breed my pain?
    And wilt thou not restore my joys again?
 Music in Simpson, pp. 225–31.

[OLD MERRYTHOUGHT *admits* MERCHANT]

OLD MERRYTHOUGHT
  You are welcome, sir, you are welcome. You see your
  entertainment; pray you, be merry.
MERCHANT
  Oh, Master Merrythought, I am come to ask you   245
  Forgiveness for the wrongs I offered you
  And your most virtuous son; they're infinite;
  Yet my contrition shall be more than they.
  I do confess my hardness broke his heart,
  For which just heaven hath given me punishment   250
  More than my age can carry. His wandering spirit,
  Not yet at rest, pursues me everywhere,
  Crying, 'I'll haunt thee for thy cruelty'.
  My daughter, she is gone, I know not how,
  Taken invisible, and whether living   255
  Or in grave, 'tis yet uncertain to me.
  Oh Master Merrythought, these are the weights
  Will sink me to my grave. Forgive me, sir.
OLD MERRYTHOUGHT
  Why, sir, I do forgive you, and be merry;
  And if the wag in's lifetime played the knave,   260
  Can you forgive him too?
MERCHANT   With all my heart, sir.
OLD MERRYTHOUGHT
  Speak it again, and heartily.
MERCHANT   I do, sir,
  Now, by my soul, I do.
OLD MERRYTHOUGHT [*sings*]
     With that came out his paramour;
     She was as white as the lily flower,   265
     Hey, troll, trolly, lolly.

Enter LUCE *and* JASPER

     With that came out her own dear knight,
     He was as true as ever did fight, etc.
  Sir, if you will forgive 'em, clap their hands together; there's
  no more to be said i'th'matter.   270
MERCHANT
  I do, I do.

269 *'em* Q3 (ham Q1, Q2)
    clap strike hands together in token of betrothal
270 *said* Q2 (sad Q1)

CITIZEN

 I do not like this. – peace, boys, hear me one of you. Every-
 body's part is come to an end but Rafe's, and he's left out.

BOY

 'Tis long of yourself, sir; we have nothing to do with his
 part.   275

CITIZEN

 Rafe, come away. – Make an end on him as you have done
 of the rest, boys; come.

WIFE

 Now, good husband, let him come out and die.

CITIZEN

 He shall, Nell. – Rafe, come away quickly and die, boy.

BOY

 'Twill be very unfit he should die, sir, upon no occasion, 280
 and in a comedy too.

CITIZEN

 Take you no care of that, sir boy, is not his part at an end,
 think you, when he's dead? – Come away, Rafe.

Enter RAFE, *with a forked arrow through his head*

RAFE

 When I was mortal, this my costive corpse
 Did lap up figs and raisins in the Strand,   285
 Where sitting, I espied a lovely dame,
 Whose master wrought with lingel and with awl,
 And underground he vampèd many a boot.
 Straight did her love prick forth me, tender sprig,
 To follow feats of arms in warlike wise   290
 Through Waltham Desert, where I did perform
 Many achievements, and did lay on ground
 Huge Barbaroso, that insulting giant,

---

274 *long* on account

276 *an end* ed. (om. Q1)

283 s.d. Cf. the quarto version of *3 Henry VI* (1595): '*Enter Clifford wounded, with*
  an arrow in his neck' (II.vi.0 s.d.).
  forked barbed

284 ff. The speech parodies ghost scenes from several plays, including *Richard III*
  (V.iii.124), and the beginning of *The Spanish Tragedy*; it also contains echoes of
  Quicksilver's 'Repentance' in *Eastward Ho* (1605), V.v.49 ff.

284 *costive* slow, constipated

287 *lingel* shoemaker's waxed thread

288 *vampèd* renewed the uppers of

293 *insulting* bragging

And all his captives soon set at liberty.
Then honour pricked me from my native soil   295
Into Moldavia, where I gained the love
Of Pompiona, his beloved daughter,
But yet proved constant to the black-thumbed maid
Susan, and scorned Pompiona's love.
Yet liberal I was, and gave her pins   300
And money for her father's officers.
I then returnèd home, and thrust myself
In action, and by all men chosen was
Lord of the May, where I did flourish it,
With scarfs and rings, and posy in my hand.   305
After this action, I preferrèd was,
And chosen city captain at Mile End,
With hat and feather and with leading-staff,
And trained my men and brought them all off clear
(Save one man that berayed him with the noise).   310
But all these things I Rafe did undertake
Only for my belovèd Susan's sake.
Then coming home, and sitting in my shop
With apron blue, Death came unto my stall
To cheapen *aqua vitae*; but ere I   315
Could take the bottle down and fill a taste,
Death caught a pound of pepper in his hand,
And sprinkled all my face and body o'er,
And in an instant vanishèd away.

CITIZEN
    'Tis a pretty fiction i'faith.   320

RAFE
    Then took I up my bow and shaft in hand,
    And walked into Moorfields to cool myself;
    But there grim cruel Death met me again,
    And shot this forkèd arrow through my head,
    And now I faint. Therefore be warned by me,   325

---

297 *his* the Prince of Moldavia's

305 *posy* Q1ᶜ (Poesie Q1ᵘ) a motto inscribed in a ring

306 *preferrèd* promoted

308 *leading-staff* officer's baton

310 *berayed him* befouled himself

315 *cheapen* bargain for

322 *Moorfields* north of the city wall, between Bishopsgate and Cripplegate; in 1606
    they were laid out in walks and became a popular summer resort

My fellows every one, of forkèd heads.
Farewell, all you good boys in merry London;
Ne'er shall we more upon Shrove Tuesday meet
And pluck down houses of iniquity –
My pain increaseth. – I shall never more   330
Hold open, whilst another pumps both legs,
Nor daub a satin gown with rotten eggs;
Set up a stake! – Oh, never more I shall.
I die; fly, fly, my soul, to Grocers' Hall!
Oh, oh, oh, etc.   335

WIFE
Well said, Rafe. Do your obeisance to the gentlemen and go
your ways. Well said, Rafe.

Exit RAFE

OLD MERRYTHOUGHT
Methinks all we, thus kindly and unexpectedly reconciled,
should not depart without a song.
MERCHANT
A good motion.   340
OLD MERRYTHOUGHT
Strike up, then.

Song

Better music ne'er was known
Than a choir of hearts in one.
Let each other that hath been
Troubled with the gall or spleen,   345
Learn of us to keep his brow
Smooth and plain as ours are now.

326 *forkèd heads* of cuckolds
328 *Shrove Tuesday* The prentices traditionally revelled and rioted on Shrove
   Tuesday before Lent; see Brand, ii. 53 ff., Laroque, pp. 93–103, and Introduction, pp. xxi–iii.
331 *Hold ... legs* cf. the Induction to Jonson's *Bartholomew Fair*: 'would not a fine
   pump upon the stage ha' done well for a property now? And a punk set under
   upon her head, with her stem upward, and ha' been soused by my witty young
   masters o' the Inns o' Court?' (31–4)
332 *satin gown* worn by dandies
333 *Set ... stake* to which a cock would be tied on Shrove Tuesday and then stoned
   to death (Laroque, p. 97)
339 *depart* take leave of one another
343 *one* unison

Sing, though before the hour of dying;
He shall rise, and then be crying,
'Hey, ho, 'tis nought but mirth,   350
That keeps the body from the earth'.

Exeunt OMNES

Epilogus

CITIZEN
Come, Nell, shall we go? The play's done.
WIFE
Nay, by my faith, George, I have more manners than so; I'll
speak to these gentlemen first. – I thank you all, gentlemen,
for your patience and countenance to Rafe, a poor fatherless child; and if I might see you at my house, it should go   5
hard but I would have a pottle of wine and a pipe of
tobacco for you; for truly, I hope you do like the youth, but
I would be glad to know the truth. I refer it to your own
discretions, whether you will applaud him or no; for I will
wink, and whilst you shall do what you will. I thank you   10
with all my heart. God give you good night. – Come,
George.

[*Exeunt*]

FINIS

6 *pottle* measure of two quarts
10 *wink* close my eyes
    whilst meanwhile

Made in the USA
San Bernardino, CA
23 February 2018